WEALTH

HOW TO BECOME SERIOUSLY RICH ON ANY INCOME

First Edition

by

David Batchelor
FHD.ALIA(dip).MSFA.CFP

All rights reserved
Witherby & Co. Ltd.
32-36 Aylesbury Street,
London EC1R 0ET

First Edition 2003

WITHERBYS
PUBLISHING

© David Batchelor 2003
ISBN 1 85609 254 2

Printed and Published by
WITHERBY & CO. LTD
32-36 Aylesbury Street
London EC1R 0ET
Tel No: 020 7251 5341   Fax No: 020 7251 1296
International Tel No: +44 20 7251 5341
International Fax No: +44 20 7251 1296
E-mail: books@witherbys.co.uk
www: witherbys.com

British Library Cataloguing in Publication Data

Batchelor, David
Wealth – How to become Seriously Rich on any Income
1 Title
ISBN 1 85609 254 2

Contents

Introduction   v

About the Author   viii

Chapter 1   The Why   1

Chapter 2   Building your own Personal Belief System   9

Chapter 3   Goals & Targets   21

Chapter 4   The How   31

Chapter 5   Short-term Goals   35

Chapter 6   Protection   43

Chapter 7   Savings   53

Chapter 8   More Savings   61

Chapter 9   Pound Cost Averaging and the Magic
                 of Compound Interest   73

Chapter 10   Investing   81

Chapter 11   More Investing   103

Chapter 12   Accelerating Your Plan   123

Chapter 13   Destroying Debt   131

Chapter 14   Summary   141

Foreword

David Batchelor has put into words a concise, simple, step by step plan, which if followed, will ensure financial security.

There is nothing new in this book. It contains everything that financially sophisticated people have always known. But never before has it been laid out in such a simple, easy to follow, step by step approach to accumulating personal wealth.

It does not promise intense wealth or overnight success. It breaks down all the steps, starting at the very beginning with the question "why?" Why should we want to achieve financial independence? This sounds like a rhetorical question, but only when we make achieving financial independence a priority, when we believe it's not just possible but essential, can it become a reality.

But there are no quick fixes. From the "why" the book moves to the "how". These are the positive steps, which if followed, will ensure results over the long term.

This book deserves to be read by every responsible earner for if we all followed its precepts, our society would surely be a happier place.

Over 400 years ago, Francis Bacon wrote "the measure of a man's fortune lies in his own hands". David Batchelor's book shows how Francis Bacon can be proved right and how it can be achieved.

Tony Gordon
Past President – Life Insurance Association
Past President – Million Dollar Round Table
Past Board Member – Personal Investment Authority

Introduction

Doug

So you want to be Wealthy?

It's what everyone says, they want to be wealthy, rich, or a millionaire, and yet I'm not so sure. It is so simple to become wealthy, anyone can do it, but for some strange reason the majority of people do not.

In my business I have seen thousands of people, rich and poor, wealthy and hard up, and when you first look at them its hard to see why there is such a difference between them. There are intelligent wealthy people as well as poor intelligent people. There are wealthy people who are clearly not the 'sharpest tools in the box' as well as those who are finding it hard to get by. OK, you have the lady who married into money, or the man who inherited a fortune, but I am not talking about these people. I am talking about the self-made. The person who started with nothing and became a millionaire. The person who, against all the odds, without any training, without any 'luck', has become seriously wealthy. It is through the study of these people, the techniques that they use and the beliefs that they have that I have put together what I believe is the *guaranteed* way to become seriously wealthy.

Now you must understand that the techniques explained in this book are simple, and work for everyone who uses them, but that does not make them easy. You cannot expect to become seriously wealthy without some form of commitment and some work. What you need to do you may find hard, because it means doing things differently from how you have done before. Remember the definition of madness is 'doing the same thing over and over again and expecting different results'. So if you are not wealthy now, I suggest you do not do what you have been doing any more.

You need a new plan, a new set of goals, a new set of beliefs and guiding principles, otherwise nothing will change. Are you prepared to make some small but significant changes to your life, your goals and finances? Because if you are not you might as well put this book down and continue to watch TV and hope to win the lottery, because that will be the only way you will become wealthy. However, if you are prepared to spend about 2 to 3 hours reading this book, and an hour reviewing your finances and about an hour per week working these plans then you can become seriously wealthy, even on your salary.

How this book is set out

The book is divided into two parts, each part forming a crucial part of what you need to know to become seriously wealthy.

The first part of the book is called **The WHY**. This part concerns itself with:

- why people become wealthy

- why people do not become wealthy

- what financial wealth really is

- what goals you need to have and how to set them

In effect it deals with the psychological aspects of becoming wealthy. Now I know that, if you are like me, you will want to get into the 'nitty gritty' of what to do with your finances, but you will be making the same mistakes I made before I knew any better.

You *must* have a strong enough 'why', to make 'the how' work, otherwise, you will not succeed. It is this 'why' that we must work on, so that 'the how' works.

The second part of the book is **THE HOW**.

This is an area where many people I know have gone wrong, and it is thought that just having the right goals and attitude is enough. They think that a positive mental attitude will bring them through and let them achieve all those things they want, but this is not the case. You can have all the attitudes and goals that you want, but at the end of the day you still have to do something. Only your action will change your circumstances. As the saying goes, 'the man at the top of the mountain did not fall there', and so you need some techniques.

Now this is where you may get worried, but don't. Every one of the techniques and plans in this book are simple and work. They only require that you do them. You do not need to be a financial genius or have a degree in mathematics, you simply need to have read **The Why**. If you have and have done what that section instructs then you can complete **The How**. And, if you complete **The How**, and do what it instructs, then you will become seriously wealthy, even on your income.

Instructions

You need to *read all the book in the order that it is written* for it to work properly. I have spent a great deal of time looking at many other systems for becoming 'rich' and spent an even greater amount of time working with my clients to 'test' the systems that are explained in this book. What I have found is that you need to do things in a particular order for them to work.

You see, if I say "dog bites man" it means one thing, but if I say "man bites dog" it means something entirely different and yet I have used the same words, but simply changed the order and sequence, or the syntax. The sequence in which you do the things in the book is more important than it first appears. Every part of the book is built on the previous part. This is how this book works. If you jump straight into the second section on **The How** you will have some success, but it will not last because you have not built the foundation that is required for you to succeed in the long term and so you will sabotage your results sooner or later.

Also, if you only work through the first section **The Why**, then you will again have some success, but the results will take a long time to come, and you will probably get bored along the way. So, **please, please,**

please take the time to read through the entire book, without skipping, including completing any tasks along the way. If you do these simple things you will not only be amazed at the results, but you will be astounded at what you can achieve in a relatively short period of time.

If you continue to work the techniques described in this book you will, I guarantee, become seriously wealthy, even on your salary.

SO, lets get started and do what needs to be done!

About the Author

David Batchlor has been a Director of Wills & Trust Independant Financial Planning Ltd, since 1994 when the company was established, specialising in work mainly with business owners and entrepreneurs and the more mature client wishing to invest both for capital growth and income. Prior to this he was a senior financial consultant with Canada Life and Commerical Union. David is well qualified with F.H.D., A.L.I.A. (dip)., M.S.F.A.

Vocational accomplisments include being a qualifier for MDRT and MDRT Court of the Table as well as being voted Chairman for the Regional Life Insurance Assocation.

As well as being a speaker for the Life Insurance Association on business and practice management, he is a speaker on business management and legal issues for The Wills Register and regularly speaks on business taxation and investment issues at seminars.

He is the Chairman for the RISK Share and Investment Club.

Privately, David is a family man married to Helen with two children, Emily and Hope. Since moving from London in 1987 he has resided in Aylesbury.

Chapter 1   The WHY

To become wealthy the greatest requirement that you must have is a "why" which will give you the persistence to continue when things go wrong. The "why" will give you the strength to go outside your comfort zone and do something that you have not done before. The "why" will generate energy within you to achieve what you want both on a financial level and a personal level. If you do not have a "why" then *you will fail* in your attempt to be wealthy by your own efforts.

Having a "why" is only half the story. You must make that "why" into something that absorbs you, something that inspires you, something that you truly believe in. It must become something that is ingrained in your belief system to such a degree that you do not question either your ability or desire to become wealthy.

In this part of the book we will be doing the following:

• Building and discovering your own personal "why"

- Build your "why" into part of your belief system

- Discovering what being wealthy really means

- Setting your goals to become wealthy

It is important to understand why so many people are not wealthy. If you can understand what is going wrong, it will make it easier for you to see what must be done to put it right. After all , if it is so easy to be wealthy, why are so many people struggling to make ends meet, or simply comfortable with their lot.

There are basically 10 reasons why people are not wealthy. Understanding these problems and pitfalls will help you to avoid them and, more importantly, build your "why". BUT before you look over the page I want you to make a list of what you might think are the 10 reasons why people are not wealthy. Now it is important that you do this. If you do not you will not start the process that installs the required belief system in you, and you will get to the end of the book asking why it does not work for you. So, go and get a pen and *write a list of 10 reasons why people are not wealthy.*

---

10 reasons why people are not wealthy

1.

2.

3.

4.

5.

6.

7.

8.

9.

10.

Is the box full?, have you really written 10 reasons? if not, do not go on, please take 30 seconds to jot them down, it's not a big time investment, is it? If you won't do this, you certainly won't do what you need to do to become seriously wealthy.

So then, what are the 10 reasons?

1. They never clearly define wealth

Imagine for a moment that you are an archer in the next Olympics. You are lined up with the other great archers of the world. You have spent thousands of hours practising and now is your big moment. Its your turn and you lift up the bow and pull back. There is only one problem, there is no target. Now what is the chance of hitting a bullseye. NIL. If you do not have a target you cannot hit it!

Money is the same as archery. If you do not know what wealth is, especially to you, how on earth do you think you can reach that goal.

The solution

Define what wealth is in your own terms.

2. They make wealth a moving target

You're back in the Olympics again, but now you've got your target. You lift the bow again and pull back. The problems is that someone keeps moving the target and what's worse they keep moving it further away. As soon as you eye up the bull it all changes.

This is what many people do. As soon as they get close to becoming wealthy, they change the target, they move the goal posts. Consequently, it becomes impossible to reach.

The solution

Set your goals correctly so that they do not need to be changed

3. They define wealth in ways that make it impossible to achieve

It would be easy to say that to be really wealthy you need to have £1 billion in cash, in your bank account, on instant access and that if you did not have that, then this book does not work. But this is simply a fallacy. You see, wealth is different to us all and to most people it is considerably less than £1 billion. However, if you are a millionaire, you might need a billion to be considered wealthy, in which case it would be all right for you to describe wealth that way.

The solution

We must set our financial goals on a realistic and calculable basis. We must ensure that the goals are the right ones for us and nobody else.

4. They do not believe that they can be wealthy

I think that this is probably the greatest single reason why people are not wealthy. Unless you believe something then it is virtually impossible to make it happen. If you do not believe that you can be wealthy, then your subconscious will act to ensure that you are not and it will stop you from being wealthy more effectively than any crash in the stock market.

The mind can be likened to an iceberg, one tenth, the conscious part, is above water and we are aware if it. We can control what happens and what it does. However, the other nine tenths are under water, this is the subconscious mind. This is the part of the mind that instructs your legs to move when you walk. It reminds your heart to beat, even when you are asleep. It files the faces of people that you know in your memory for easy retrieval, and, most important of all, it tells you what you are really capable of.

The solution

We must build a belief system that will convince both your conscious and subconscious mind that you can be wealthy.

5. They don't make wealth a must

Many people would 'like' to be wealthy. They think it is a good idea and just as soon as they finish watching the TV they might get around to doing something about it. It is not enough to want to be wealthy, it must become a must in your life. It must become like your desire for food, water and air. It must become a condition by which you measure your success. It must be something that would be so painful not to achieve that you could not possibly contemplate not achieving it.

The solution

When building your belief system you must build your desire for wealth to the point that it becomes wealth.

6. They don't have a plan

I know that it is hard to believe, but some people actually go through life without making a financial plan ! Can you believe it ? These people will spend months organising their holidays, but do not take the time to plan and organise their finances !

When you take the time to think about it, it is ludicrous to expect, or even hope to get wealthy without making a plan, but this is how most people spend their financial lives.

The solution

Make a plan.

7. They don't do what the plan tells them to do

Have you ever made a new years resolution and not followed through? Surely, its not worth the time making a resolution, unless your are going to keep to it? But this is what happens and this is one reason why people do not get wealthy. They have great intentions and put together a beautiful plan. But what happens when they get a lump sum of cash? Do they invest it? Do they save it? Do they use the 50/50 system recommended in this book? No, they spend it and say, well I'll deal with it properly next time.

Now, the problem with plans is that, if you don't action it once, it becomes much easier not to action it a second time and even easier not to action it a third. All because of the iceberg in your head.

The solution

Set up a realistic plan that you can keep to AND KEEP TO IT.

8 They don't take responsibility

That iceberg in your head is back again. Whenever you blame somebody else for your bad luck, your subconscious believes you and re-reinforces that belief. When a similar set of circumstances comes along, it reminds you of what happens next time and you don't even try because someone else will work against you and you will not succeed.

You see, if you do not take responsibility for your circumstances, and it is all everybody else's fault, how can you do anything about it. Only the person responsible can affect the result and so you must accept responsibility – absolutely!

The solution

You must build a belief system that puts you in control.

9. They give up when things get tough

Winston Churchill said, in a famous address: "Never, Never, Never give up". Now why would you not take the great man's advice? It is all too easy to give up when things go wrong, when markets turn against you, when the tax man calls, but to do so will lead to failure. The iceberg will both help and hinder you. If you give up on some small challenge, then it will reinforce the give up attitude. It will make it that much easier to give up next time. If, however, you do not give up and forge ahead, then the reverse happens. You condition your mind to find ways to win, this then makes the next challenge easier and the next one easier still. Have you not found this to be true? Do you not look back on things which used to cause you problems and think how small and insignificant they are now?

The solution

Develop the plan that provides for challenges, and build a belief system that will not let you give up.

10. They do not get good coaching

If you wanted to build a brick wall would you go to a nurse to ask her advice? If you had a strange purple and green rash appear on your knee would you ask your plumber for his advice? If you had you car breakdown would you call a grocer? No, then why take financial advice from someone who is not qualified to give it.

DO NOT take advice from anyone who is not qualified to give it. Why take advice from a newspaper journalist who, last week may have been the sports columnist, and where you have not investor protection? Do not listen to a friend's get rich quick idea, as it will probably be them who is getting rich quicker.

Instead listen to those people who know what they are talking about. Do not get hung up on their charges, or what commission they may get paid, get hung up on the quality of their advice. It is this that counts.

The solution

Find an excellent, qualified adviser and use them when required.

Chapter 2   Building Your Own Personal Belief System

There is only one prerequisite for becoming wealthy and that is, believing that you can become wealthy. This is the only prerequisite. Everyone, absolutely everyone, who is wealthy, believed that they could become wealthy before they became wealthy. It is an absolute requirement that you are totally convinced that you can become wealthy. If you do not, or if you harbour some small trace of doubt, then you will definitely not become wealthy.

Now, believing that you will become wealthy is a major advantage, but not necessarily a requirement. But, as we are going to build your belief system we might as well build it so that you will believe you will become wealthy.

Why are beliefs so important?

The way in which we act, the way in which people act towards us, and many of the circumstances that arise in our lives are a direct result of our belief system.

We cannot always control what happens to us, but we can always control how we act towards it. This is what Dr Stephen Covey, in his excellent book *'The seven habits of highly effective people'* calls proactivity.

Think of yourself in a boat. When the wind is behind, you simply sail along with it and let it carry you. But what do you do when the wind blows against you? Do you close your sails and wait for the direction to change? Do you keep you sail up and let it blow you backwards? Of course not! When you are battling against the wind you learn to tack into the wind. In effect, you use the keel of the boat to slice through the water at a cross angle to the wind and therefore if the wind blows against you, you can still sail into it.

This is how we must make our lives. It's not what happens to you that's important, it's the way that you deal with it. Every successful and wealthy person has had set backs and problems, the difference is that they have learnt how to deal with them, perhaps even how to turn them into an advantage. How do you do this? It's done by having the right belief system. It is your belief system that will control your actions more than any other single factor. It is your actions that will make you seriously wealthy, even on your salary.

How do you change your belief system?

In 1920 Emile Coue, a French Pharmacist developed a method of autosuggestion that became known as Coueism. You will probably know of his work by the more popular term 'The Placebo' effect. Coue discovered, almost by accident, the power of belief. Faced with a stubborn patient who would not take no for an answer, he recommended a new drug. The patient took the pill and a few days later returned delighted saying that he was fully recovered. In fact, Coue had simply given him a sugar pill. However, because the patient believed that he was being given a new effective drug, his body acted in such a way as if it had received a drug. In reality it was simply the power of his mind that was making the changes.

Coue took this method further and after research found that simple autosuggestion had the same effect as the placebo effect. To test this he had patients repeat positive phrases three times a day. In this case Coue used the words:

"Everyday, in every way I'm becoming better and better"

Coue found that patients had recognisable physiological changes from the simple repeating of this phrase.

Since his work many other researchers and psychologists have found that the use of particular phases can affect peoples' belief systems. Hypnotherapists from Milton Ericson to the TV Hypnotist and therapist Paul McKenna have used similar techniques to change peoples' belief systems in both waking and trance states.

'The workings of the mind' is an interesting area of study, but as a book about becoming wealthy lets get straight to the action. We do not need to know how something works to use it. Indeed most of us do not understand electricity, but are willing to throw a switch to get light.

We will come back to exactly what you should do shortly, but lets now consider what we want to put into our belief system.

What should I believe?

In their book *'How to think like a millionaire – The success secrets of ten millionaires'* Charles-Albert Poissant and Christian Godefrey said:

"You will never get rich if you can't picture yourself rich"

And they are absolutely right.

We must develop one absolute belief. That we can become wealthy. It will then be of immeasurable benefit to build a belief that we will become wealthy. In fact, why not build a belief that we must become wealthy.

It is these three beliefs that we must install into our subconscious if we want to achieve real wealth. We must be absolutely convinced that we CAN become wealthy, we WILL become wealthy and that we *MUST* become wealthy.

We must work in two areas. Firstly we must work on the conscious mind and overcome our own limiting beliefs. We must do this in a way that will build the right beliefs in our subconscious mind. Now, we have already begun this process in the last chapter, but now we will take it further.

This is when you need to do a little work.

The next section will take about 30 to 40 minutes to complete. You will need an alarm clock, a plain postcard, a pen and paper, and a quiet room. I recommend that you complete this section on your own, without any form of interruption. Take time to complete the exercises fully. It is important that you really work at them, that you put in every ounce of effort that you can. Now remember, this is for your benefit. You are the one who will benefit from doing this properly. Also you will be the one who will LOOSE OUT if you do not follow this through. So commit yourself and get stuck in.

Exercise One

Starting in the box below you are now going to write out all the advantages to being wealthy. Take a clock, and time yourself. Write for **no less** than 5 minutes. I need you to write continuously and list every possible benefit from being wealthy. Set you clock and get ready to write.

NOW LIST EVERY BENEFIT YOU CAN THINK OF TO BEING WEALTHY.

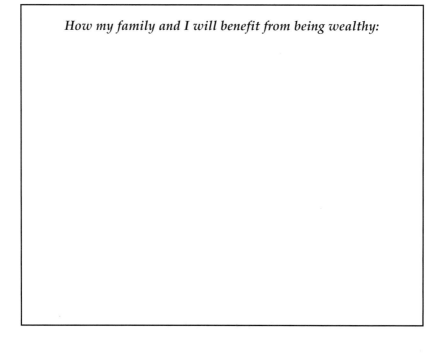

How my family and I will benefit from being wealthy:

Have you written for a minimum of 5 minutes? If not go back and finish off. It is *absolutely essential* that you complete this exercise.

How my family and I will benefit from being wealthy (cont.):

Now that you have finished how many have you got? 10, 15, 20. If you have not got 50 then go back and think of some more. What about those you can help by being wealthy? What charities could you support? Who in the family could you help? How could you help your children in their lives? Or your grandchildren? Just think if you were wealthy and could pass that to your children's children's children, you would be the one they would remember. What could you buy, what gifts could you make, what business could you support? Where could you go? What goals could you achieve?

Have you listed 50 reasons, if not go back and keep going until you do.

Exercise two

Now I want you to think about how you would feel if you were wealthy. I want you to think about all those people you are going to help, how great that will make you feel. Think about the type of house you will have, the car you will drive. Think about the security that you will have and what security you can pass down to your family. Think how happy you are going to be.

Now set the alarm clock for 5 minuets and then close you eyes, lean back in your chair and really feel how you would feel, picture yourself being wealthy and tell yourself how great and secure and comforting it feels.

How did that feel? Could you really picture yourself as wealthy? Did you really take the time to do the exercise, remember, this is for your benefit. If you do not take action then nothing will change.

Exercise Three

Now I want you to write again. This time I want you to think of all the disadvantages of not being wealthy. I want you to write at least 50 disadvantages of being poor. What will you not be able to achieve? Who will you not be able to help? What will you not be able to do?

Set you clock for 5 minutes and write.

The effects on my family and me of not being wealthy are:

How many have you written. Again, if you have not written 50 then carry on until you have.

Exercise Four

Set your alarm for 5 minutes. Then I want you to sit back and think of what it will be like to have financial problems. I want you to think about the embarrassment you will suffer, how your children will feel. Think of those people that you could have helped losing out, think of all the things you and your family will not receive.

Now sit back and really imagine.

How does it feel? Not too good I should think, but unless you take action this may be you. You must, absolutely must, become wealthy.

Exercise Five

Take your blank post card and write the following on it:

"Everyday, in every way I am growing richer and richer"

Exercise five, will take you 14 days. But I'm pleased to say it should only take you about 10 seconds three times a day.

Everyday when you wake, once during the day, preferably after a meal and last thing at night I want you to read your card. If possible read it out loud with as much passion and belief as you can muster, but at the very least read it with passion in your mind. Make sure you read it, and don't just say it from memory. It is important to see as well as hear. Then very briefly think of how great it's going to feel to be wealthy.

Do this for 14 days, without missing a day. If for any reason you miss any time in those 14 days, your 14 days start over again.

Exercise six

This is the last exercise and is a request rather than an instruction. Go out to your local bookstore, or library and get hold of *'Think and grow rich'* by Napoleon Hill. Then read it.

You will find this book is a mine of information. Napoleon Hill made it his life mission to find out the characteristics of wealth. So why not read what he found out. After all, it can only help.

Chapter 3   Goals and Targets

Looking back to our reasons why people do not become wealthy you will see that the first three reasons they never clarify wealth and make wealth a moving target, therefore defining wealth in ways that are impossible to achieve, are all related to goal setting.

So let's look at them in a little more detail:

They never clarify wealth

If you do not know what wealth is, two things will happen. Firstly, you will not achieve it because you do not know what it is. Secondly, you may become wealthy, but do not know that you are wealthy, which gives rise to the same psychological problems that not being wealthy creates. In the same way that a man who can read, but does not read is no better than a man who can't read, a wealthy man who does not know that he is wealthy, is no better than a poor man.

They make wealth a moving target:

It's one thing to hit a goal, but it is another to try to hit a moving target. If you were a marksman, you would not want to make your task harder by swinging the target on a rope, so why do the same with your financial goals? The process of goal setting and in particular actually writing your goals down, makes the target easier to hit. You should avoid, at all costs, moving the goals posts.

They define wealth in ways that make it impossible to achieve

I am a positive thinker, a 'half full' person, but I understand what should be considered possible and what cannot. If you are 65 years old, overweight, smoke cigarettes, and have not taken exercise for the last ten years you will not run a marathon in under four hours, no matter how positive you are. If you're only earning £15,000 per year, then you will not become a billionaire without massively changing your circumstances. Many people set such incredibly difficult goals, in such short time scales, that they are certain to fail.

Avoiding these three mistakes is what we are going to acheive in this chapter. As before, unless you fully take part in each exercise you will be wasting your time. BUT, if you take the time to do the exercises, which should take about an hour or so, then you will have taken a giant leap towards being wealthy. Not only that, but something special will happen. Once you have completed the exercises you will begin to see the light at the end of the tunnel. You will start to glimpse how simple it may be to be wealthy. This, I think you will find will drive you on to the second section of this book – **The How**.

What is wealthy? And what is seriously wealthy?

Wealth means different things to many people. To some it may mean being able to pay all the bills on time, to others it may mean a yacht, to others it may mean owning their own home. But what is it to you? It is different to each of us. However, we can, by working through a few exercises calculate the true figure of wealth for each of us. The process will be the same for each person, but the figures will be different for each person. You may also find that the figures change over time. Usually the figures will grow because of inflation and your increased desires, but I have known it to fall in some cases. For this reason it is important to review the figures each year, I recommend doing this in December. Its a great time to measure your achievements over the year and to review your targets for the coming year. If you add this process to an end of year review it will help spur you on as well as up-date your figures.

So then, what is wealthy? And what is seriously wealthy?

WEALTHY

Imagine for one moment being able to live your existing lifestyle without relying on anyone else in the world. You would not need your employer if you are employed, or your customers if you run your own business. You would be able to live in your present home, or one similar, drive the same car, take the same number and type of holidays, buy the family the same presents. When you are wealthy you would live from your own personal resources. Your income comes solely from the value and yields of your assets. This is wealth!

Wealthy means being able to maintain your present standard of living purely from the income of your own assets. In the UK there are less than 5% of the population who can do this. Virtually everyone depends on their income to support them. Wealthy people don't. They know that they are totally financially independent. That do not rely on any one else for their standard of living. Now, they may continue to work, and most financially independent people do, but the point is that they do not have to work, they choose to work. So from now on we shall refer to wealthy as Financially Independent, as this is what real wealth is.

SERIOUSLY WEALTHY

Seriously wealthy people go one step further, a seriously wealthy person has enough money to do exactly what they want, whenever they want as much as they want for as long as they want. This means they have total freedom financially. Again this does not necessarily mean that they will be jetting off all over the world, it just means that they can. Seriously wealthy people have enough personal assets so that the income from those assets will not only support them in their present life style, but they can enhance their lifestyle to fulfil their wants and desires. In effect, they are financially free. They have both the capital and income to be free of all financial worries and from now on we shall call being seriously wealthy, Financial Freedom as this truly defines the seriously wealthy state. By thinking of Financial Freedom we will conjure up a more realistic view of what we want to achieve.

Although we have done a great deal of good work in the preceding chapters, we must continue to work on our subconscious mind. Changing wealthy to financially independent and seriously wealthy to Financially Free we will be sending the right signals to our subconscious. If you think about it, you don't really care if your are wealthy or not, you care about what being wealthy can do for you So from now on we will think of, and plan for, being Financially Independent and Financially Free.

Calculating Financial Independence

First you must do some research. It means putting together a budget. The idea of the budget is to get a fix on what your true outgoings are. List below your annual expenses for the following:

- mortgage/rent payments (interest only for mortgages, do not include capital repayment or endowment policies)

- local government tax/rates

- utility bills(include telephone, gas electric, water and oil)

- household expenditure(include food, toiletries, clothing etc.)

- holiday costs

- motoring costs

- insurance costs(for car, house and life)

- entertainment/spending money

Now total these up and you will have your net required income on an annual basis to maintain your existing standard of living. This is the amount that you must be able to generate from assets to be totally financially independent. If your assets produced this as an income each year, then you would not need to work to maintain your standard of living. Do not at this stage concern yourself with the effects of inflation, we will deal with this in section two of the book.

We now know the level of income that is needed to be financially free we must find out how much capital we need to generate this amount of income annually. But before we can do his we must find out your view towards investment risk and reward. What does this mean? Each person has their own tolerance for risking their own money when investing. I, for example, have quite a high level of tolerance. I am comfortable with seeing the level of my investments rise and fall over the days, months and years. Many of my clients, however, do not want to risk any capital, they want to protect the level of capital and want to grow their assets with the simple addition of interest. Once we know your view towards investment risk we can ascertain a likely return for your capital based on historical data. This figure can then be used to calculate the level of capital that you require to generate sufficient income to become Financially Independent and Financially Free.

Now this is where, if you are using a financial adviser, I suggest you seek their help. They will speak with you to ascertain your view towards investment reward and risk, and from this will be able to provide a level of return annually that is in line with your view towards risk and reward. However, if you do not yet have an adviser, lets work through a simple method of calculating your acceptable risk level. Now, this is not the ideal way to calculate your view towards investment risk, it is simply a generalised barometer that you can use until you find a financial adviser that you feel comfortable with.

Imagine a staircase with ten steps.

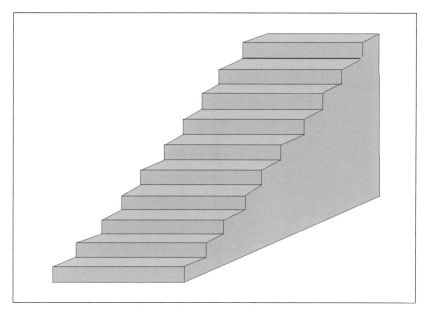

Investing is very much like standing on these steps. The higher you stand the further you can see and the more exciting the view. However, the higher you are the greater the chance of hurting yourself if you should fall. The lower you are the less well you can see but the safer you are if you should fall. This is the case with investments. Adventurous investments can give outstanding returns, but at the same time may hurt if the investment fails. Low risk investments act as they sound. They give a steady low rate of return but will usually protect your capital.

On our staircase the first step will be *holding cash*. You can only lose it if its stolen or inflation eats it away. The second step would be a *bank account*, and the third a *building society account*. On the tenth step, the *lottery* would be sitting alone. It gives either massive returns or no return at all depending on whether you win or not. The ninth step would be *futures* and *options* where again great amounts can be won or lost. Individual *shares* would be on the eighth step. The steps in between would be populated with various other *investments* where the level of risk increases the higher you go.

Now decide, where you would sit if you could only choose one step. We all know that we would all like to be spread between a number of steps, but in this instance you can't, you can only choose one step. Which one would it be? Don't get hung up on the different products or investment vehicles, just think of the level. Are you adventurous in life? Do you like to take a risk? Are you the sort of person who will go on holiday by booking a flight without knowing where you will stay

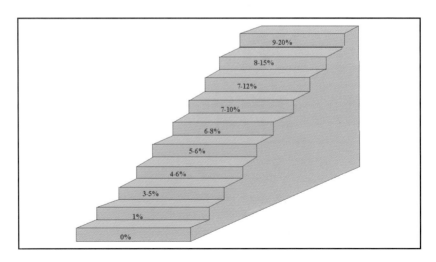

that night? If so, you will be high up the scale perhaps on the 7th or 8th step. Alternatively, you may be a cautious person. The sort of person who does not like to go out of their comfort zone. You probably drive a sensible car and plan your holidays in detail. You probably keep a tight control on your finances and know exactly what is in your account at all times. If this is the case you will be lower down the staircase, perhaps a 3, 4 or 5. None of the steps is incorrect. There is no perfect place to be, there is only the right level for you, so don't seek other peoples opinions, just note where you are.

Now you have chosen your step, look at the diagram below and you will find a figure. This figure is the average return that someone with that view towards investment risk could expect to receive over a five year average. Some years it would be higher, and some lower. Indeed, if you were on step 7 or above some years you would loose money. Remember this is the average.

Let's assume for the exercise that you are Mr or Mrs Average. If so your will choose step 5. This means that you will, on average, receive a return of up to 6% per year.

Now for the maths. Take your required income and insert it into the following equation:

$$\frac{\text{INCOME REQUIRED}}{\text{PERCENTRAGE}} \times 100 = \text{CAPITAL REQUIRED}$$

To help you if you are not a 'figures' person here is an example.

You are Mr or Mrs Average. As such you are on step 5 and will receive, on average, 6% from your investments. As Mr or Mrs Average you will require an income of, say £20,000 per year. The formula is as follows:

$$\frac{£20,000}{6} \times 100 = £333,333$$

As you can see from the figures above, Mr or Mrs Average will require a capital sum of £333,333 to produce an income of £20,000. This means that if you had £333,333 held in an investment that returns 6% per year then you would have sufficient income from that investment to continue to retain the same standard of living as you are at present without relying on any other person. You would be Financially Independent.

If you have taken the time to do this exercise you will probably be like 90% of the people I do the exercise with. You will find firstly, that the level of income is slightly lower than you may have expected, and secondly that the level of capital required is usually much lower than expected.

Many times I have done this exercise with people who calculate enormous figures for financial independence. For example, I had one client who was earning £30,000 per year say, when I asked him how much money he would need to feel comfortable and financially independent he said, "at least £1 million". He thought that financial independence was such a high goal that he never even tried to start to work towards it. However, when we worked through the figures he only required an income of £26,000 per year to be financially independent and based on his view towards investment risk he only needed £305,882 in capital. This is less than a third of the figure that he had originally thought necessary. Immediately, it made the goal much easier to achieve, and perhaps more importantly, generated the enthusiasm to start working towards that goal.

That's Financially Independent, what about being Financially Free?

Remember Financially Free means being able to do whatever you want, whenever you want as often as you want. This means we must engage the part of our brain that will let us dream. We must think about all of those things that we listed down in the previous chapter. We must look at all the places we wanted to visit, the things we wanted to buy and the people we wanted to help.

So lets take our earlier list and have some fun with it. Repeat the figures from the list below:

Mortgage Balance	Monthly Mortgage Payment (Based on 8% interest only)
£100,000	£666
£250,000	£1666
£500,000	£3330
£750,000	£5000

- mortgage/rent payments (interest only for mortgages, do not include capital repayment or endowment policies)
- local government tax/rates
- utility bills(include telephone, gas electric, water and oil)
- household expenditure(include food, toiletries, clothing etc.)
- holiday costs
- motoring costs
- costs (for car, house and life)
- entertainment/spending money

Look at the first figure for your mortgage or rent. Now imagine that you had your ideal house. If you have done the previous exercises you will know exactly what it will be like. Now ask yourself a question. How much would it cost? Once you have put a figure on it, then, from the chart below, add to your list a note of the mortgage cost to own such a house:

If you lived in this house you would obviously be paying greater local government taxes greater household cost bills and larger utility. Estimate the level of these. These figures do not have to be accurate, just within a ballpark amount. Once you have started on your road to financial independence you can research the accurate figures and recalculate the sums involved. It is important, however, to do the basic ground work now to give your subconscious something to work on.

Next, think about holidays. From your previous lists, where did you mention you wanted to go, how long do you want to stay there, and how often do you want to go! Do you want two holidays a year or four? Will you stay away for just two weeks or three? Really think about what you would like, then estimate a cost. If you usually spend £1,500 on your annual summer holiday, perhaps you want to take two summer holidays a year and one skiing trip in the winter. This may increase your holiday costs to £6,000. Again do not get hung up on being accurate, you will find that your first rough calculation will not be far from the truth. Then add this figure to your calculations.

Next what about that car. Do you want to trade up to a £40,000 speed machine, or simply to a £25,000 MPV. You decide, and then add the costs of such a car to your calculations.

Lastly, and in some cases most importantly, entertainment/spending money. What things have you always wanted, and how much will they cost? How much WAM money (Walking About Money) do you want? How much do you want to spend on meals out, how much on trips to the theatre, to concerts etc? Let your mind dream and make a list how much they might cost. For some people you may need only £1000 per month, to others you may need £10,000. It all depends on what you want.

Now, as before, total the expenditure up and calculate the capital required based on your view towards investment risk.

I think you will find that, while you will have a large capital sum in front of you, that sum will not be as big as you had previously thought it might be. In fact, for many people they find that the figure is substantially lower than the amount that they may previously have imagined.

So there we have it! You now have two very specific levels of capital that you need to build to produce Financial Independence and Financial Freedom. For many of you, you will be surprised to find that you are already financially independent or financially free. If so, congratulations! For others, it may be a long way from the end of the journey, but as Confucius said "each journey begins with the first step", and for many people this will be the first step.

By specifically stating what we mean by being financially independent and financially free, we are doing two things.

Firstly, we are putting a specific goal in place. This goal is very specific and as such will help us to avoid the problems associated with failing.

Secondly, we are programming our subconscious. By doing the previous exercises you will have found that you had a great level of excitement and expectation to move further on to develop wealth. In effect we were opening our mind ready to receive these goals. The subconscious mind now has something specific to work on. It has a concrete goal to achieve. It is this subconscious mind that will not let you down. If you have genuinely worked each of the examples and not merely given them lip service, then you will be ready to move onto the second section of this book – THE HOW.

Chapter 4   The HOW

You have now spent three to four hours getting to this point. You have worked through the techniques to develop the subconscious side of Financial Independence, and worked through your first basic goals for Financial Independence and Financial Freedom. If you have not worked through these sections please, please, please go back and do them. Its no good simply reading how to get wealthy if you don't change what you are doing and take different action from the action that you have taken (or not as the case my be) to get to this point.

So then, lets move on with the assumption that you have worked through the previous exercises. What are we going to do now?

'The HOW' is broken down into several parts, each building on the previous part. That is with the exception of the chapter on Destroying Debt. This is a stand alone chapter and can be read and acted upon in isolation. This is because this section will only be relevant to about 30%

of those reading this book. Generally, however, those that need to deal with this section **really** need to work on this section. If this is you, then please go straight to the chapter on Destroying Debt. Once you have worked through this then come back to work on the other sections in order.

Chapter 5 will deal with short-term goals. These will be the foundation of your own Financial Plan, as this is what we are going to develop throughout the rest of the book. We are going to put together a very individual plan, a map if you like, that will set out what you will be doing from next week through to next month, next year and beyond. By developing a written plan we will do two things.

Firstly it will give you a track to run on. Now this will not be cast in stone, as it will bend and move to take account of changes of circumstance.

Secondly, by having a written plan it will be more difficult to not do what you have planned. Now of course you can ignore the plan and take different action, but if you have completed the exercises earlier in the book this is unlikely. You will experience more pain by not taking the correct action than you will feel if you follow the plan.

Chapter 6 will develop a special part of the plan regarding protection. This will deal with all the 'boring' stuff in financial planning, but like learning scales when you learn an instrument, it is vital that you get the basics sorted out before you move on to the fun part.

Chapter 7 will deal with saving. This will be the backbone of most people's Financial Independence. We all have to start somewhere and we must have some capital to work with. Most people live from earned income and by redirecting a portion of this income we will develop your wealth.

Chapter 8 will help develop your saving ability more. People have often said to me that it is all very well saving but they don't have enough money at the moment and so how can they save. In this section we will look at ways of generating the money you need to build capital.

The Magic of Compound Interest and Pound Cost Averaging will be the subjects of Chapter 9. These are often overlooked and most simple systems will help us in our quest for Financial Independence. Once you truly understand how they work and more importantly, how you can use them to your advantage, you will be on your way to developing a plan that will work for you.

Chapters 10 and 11 will concentrate on investing. In this chapter we will look at the various type of investment and consider their advantages and disadvantages and build them into your Financial Plan. Even if you only use one type of investment it is important to understand how each of them works so that, as your capital builds you can become more sophisticated in your planning.

In Chapter 12 we will look at how you can seriously accelerate your Financial Plan. We will look at how you can use property or real estate ownership to develop your Financial Independence. Through using the idea of OPM (Other Peoples Money) and gearing I will show you how it is possible to become Financially Independent within 12 to 24 months, regardless of your starting point.

In Chapter 13 we deal with Destroying Debt. As I have mentioned this will usually be of use to 30% of the people reading this book. But if you are in debt then getting out of it is something vitally important. Even if you only have a mortgage, you will benefit from working through this chapter, as I will explain the advantages and disadvantages of reducing this debt and the most effective ways of doing this.

Chapter 5   Short-term Goals

This is probably one of the most forgotten areas in Financial Planning. The main reason for this is that, when you are speaking to a Financial Adviser, this part will not pay any commission and so, often those areas that do pay commission like pensions plans and savings plans, will come first. I am not saying that this is wrong, but in my opinion, once you have dealt with the protection issues which we will look at in the next chapter, these short-term goals are the single most important areas of Financial Planning.

Too many people, when they consider Financial Planning want to get onto the 'big stuff' like investments, Sipps and SSAS's, or are blinded by much of the drivel that is in the financial pages of most newspapers that proudly proclaim "you must have a CAT marked ISA" or "the best place for your money is an AVC", instead of focusing on the basics.

So what are your short term goals?

We looked in the previous chapter at the level of capital that you require to generate your desired level of income. However, it is no good having and building your capital which are essentially longer term goals unless you have taken care of the short-term goals.

Short goals are broken down into two separate areas:

A **Capital Account** and an **Income Account**.

The main reason why most financial plans don't work is that something goes wrong. You draw up this grand plan where you are going to save or invest on a regular basis and then the boiler breaks down, or you're made redundant, or the car needs replacing. or you want to spend the money on a holiday. Any one of these things may then interrupt your plans and before your know it you are back to square one. You then think, "well what's the point". Setting up a Capital Account and an Income Account will avoid these problems, in effect we are going to plan for those events that we know will happen, we just don't know when.

The Capital Account

Do you use a credit card? Do you use it for emergencies, and then have difficulty paying it back? If so, then you are not alone. Probably more than 50% of the clients I meet have run up various debts because of an unexpected emergency, or other demands on their money. To avoid this problem we need to build a Capital Account.

A Capital Account is an account which we can use to finance the emergencies that crop up. It is the financial 'Float' that will keep the debt man at bay. It will stop the problems of paying interest and other charges to your creditors.

A Capital Account is simply an emergency fund that you can draw in the event of an emergency or when you need to purchase or replace a capital item, such as a car, or TV etc.

The Capital Account is the very first thing that you must save towards, without it you will not reach Financial Independence. Once you have built your Capital Account you can work on building your Income Account.

To build your Capital Account you must take funds from your savings.

Chapter 7 will explain what you must do to save effectively. Once you have read chapter 7 then you can start to build your Capital Account, and then onto your Income Account.

How to set up a Capital Account

Money held in a Capital Account is the only 'no risk' money that you should have. All money held in the Captial Account should be held on deposit. This means that the funds are held in a bank or building society in such a way as to guarantee the capital. In the UK this means using either Building Society accounts, Bank Deposit accounts or National Savings accounts, in the US you would use either Bank Deposit accounts or certificates of deposit. The most important point is that the value of the capital is guaranteed. Now this means that the level of return that you will receive will be relatively low, but that is ok as we are only going to keep a small portion of your money here. Another important point is that the funds must be accessible within at least 7 days. You should not use any account where more notice than this is required. The last main point to consider is tax. While we do not want to be too concerned with the net growth of these funds, as we are only going to keep a small portion of your cash here, we still want to ensure that we get a reasonable return. The biggest factor in determining the return is the deduction of tax. If the basic tax rate is 20% this will have the effect of reducing a 5% return to 4%. We therefore, want to avoid paying as much tax as possible. There are two simple ways of doing this.

1: Using your full tax allowance

If you are married or have a partner then be sure to use each others tax coding where ever you can. In the UK you can earn up to a certain amount each year before you pay tax. Now, if you work and your spouse or partner does not, then your partner is unlikely to have used their tax allowance. This means that if the Capital Account is opened in their name than you can have the interest added 'gross'. This means that no tax is deducted from the interest. To do this you need to complete the inland revenue form that the bank or building society will provide.

2: Going off-shore

This sounds very grand, but is really quite simple. If you hold an account in a country that does not make a tax deduction from your account then you will have interest credited 'gross'. This means that, even if you have used up all your tax allowance, you still will not pay tax on the interest that you receive in the country where the funds are held. You will, of course, have to pay tax when the funds are returned to the UK, but at least you will have received the benefit of 'gross roll-up'. This means that you will be earning gross interest upon gross interest. As you can see from the following chart over a five or ten year period this can make a great difference. A difference that will cost you nothing to gain. If, of course, you do not bring the cash back into the UK then you will not be taxed at all. This means that you will only be taxed on those funds that you will draw on when an emergency happens, instead of being taxed on the full amount.

YEARS	ON SHORE	OFF SHORE
5	1338	1469
10	1791	2158
15	2396	3425
25	4547	7396

The above chart shows the impact of tax being deducted at source with onshore accounts. An initial investment of £1000 is made at a return of 8% pa.

To make an off shore deposit I recommend that you speak with the independent financial adviser you spoke with originally. For a small fee they will identify the most appropriate account for you as well as the most effective country to use.

Once you have opened your account you need to set a target amount for the balance. This does vary from person to person but, I suggest a figure of two to three months net income. By using a multiple of your net income the figure will vary depending on your changes in income and so be relevant to you. I recommend a cap of £10,000 as there are very few emergencies that would cost in excess of £10,000.

How to Use the Account

Now that you have set up the account and have started to deposit funds into it, how should it be used?

The Capital Account is an emergency or 'spending' account. This means that it is to be used to cover the costs of the emergencies that crop up or the capital expenditure that you are likely to want to make. The important thing, however, is how you treat the balance. Once you have made a withdrawal from the account it must then become you major creditor. This means that you must pay the amount borrowed back with interest within a set time period. Now this time period can be whatever you think is reasonable, but I suggest it should be somewhere between 6 and 36 months. For example, say you have £3000 in the account and need to pay £700 out on a household repair. You should then decide upon the term required to repay the loan, say 12 months, you should then add interest at 10%. This means that you need to pay back £770 over the next 12 months, which means that you must pay £64.16 (£770/12) per month back into your account **in addition** to your normal savings. It is vital that this is paid back as if it were a loan. After all, if you did not have the cash float you would have had to borrow the money, the only difference here is that you have borrowed the money from yourself. It is a much better idea to pay yourself back than to pay back the bank or a credit card.

Now I understand that this can all sound very administratively complicated, but if what you are doing now is not working, you have got to change something.

You can administer your account with either a simple note book or with software on your computer. It does not matter which, but you must keep accurate records to ensure that you keep to these rules. If you try and remember the details, then it will definitely not work. You must keep a written record.

Once you have a basic Capital Account in place you will stop one of the major draws on your money, and that is the interest and charges that your credit card companies and bank make. The banks and loan companies have grown into massive conglomerates because they charge so much. Its time that you took your finances into your own hands and stop this drain.

What happens once you have built you Capital Account to the required level? When you get to this point all the interest you earn must be taken from the account and used toward your other investment and wealth building projects. The first of which will be your Income Account.

What is an Income Account?

An Income Account, unlike the Capital Account, is not an account. It is the total of your medium term, accessible investments. To make up the Income Account you can use any number of different investment vehicles and savings, including the Capital Account. Many of these investments we will develop later when we discuss investments in detail.

The purpose of the Income Account is to have sufficient funds accessible to provide at least one year of net income. The total of accessible investments that are held in the Income Account have a target value of the level of income that you previously required to be Financially Independent.

In the UK less that 5% of the population have a years cash or ready money behind them. Most people live month to month, pay cheque to pay cheque. What we want to do here is build your Income Account so that you have enough cash to survive, at your present standard of living for a whole year. Can you just imagine how that would feel? Knowing that if you lose your job, or want to go on a sabbatical, that you can support your family for a year. Can you imagine what a sense of financial relief that would be? I remember specifically the day when I reached that point. It was as though a great weight had been lifted. I suddenly realised that I was not dependent on anyone else for my income for the next month, or the one after that or the one after that. I can tell you that it is a great feeling. Once you have achieved this goal you will not want to go back.

What is one years worth of income? Well one thing it is not, is one year worth of earnings. An income account consists of enough money to continue at your present standard of living for a whole year, excluding holiday expenses and savings.

Think of it this way. If you lost your job tomorrow, what would your outgoings be? They would probably be similar to you present outgoings, with the exception that you would probably reduce some areas of expenditure, such as holidays, and other capital projects like buying the new car. It's this 'net' level of income that you are looking for.

Lets take a real life example.

One client had an income of £30,000 p.a. After tax and national insurance his net income was £22,300. Of this he spent about £1800 on holidays and saved £1800, leaving £18,700.

His Income Account was made up as follows:

Capital account	£9,000
Personal Equity Plans	£7,000
Premium bonds	£1,000
Equities	£2,000

These investments totalled £19,000, which became his Income Account. This figure was noted in his records as a specific account made up of these savings and investments. Before I met him he already had these investments, but had not, in his own mind, set them aside for any purpose. In fact, he felt very uncertain about his financial future and was worried that he would be affected if he lost his job or wanted to take a sabbatical. However, once we worked through the financial planning exercise, it was clear that he was in the top 5% of people in the UK when it came to financial liquidity, it was simply that he had not thought about his finances in these terms. Immediately he saw these figures, put in this way he became a different person. You could literally see a difference in his attitude towards money and finances. He was now on the road to Financial Independence.

So then your short-term goals are:

- to create a Capital Account which holds 2 – 3 months worth of net income

- to create an Income Account which totals a one years worth of net income.

Once you have reached these two goals then you can work to create the other areas of your financial plan. **But be warned.** With the exception of the next chapter, do not be tempted to go into longer term, inaccessible investments until you have attained these goals. I know from experience that, once you learn some of the techniques that I will cover, you will be tempted to develop other ways, especially when we cover Chapter 7 of accelerating your plan. But remember, the point of the plan is to get you to being Financially Independent and Financially Free without taking undue risk. For this reason please do not be tempted to jump ahead, but continue to work through the financial plan that I am describing.

Chapter 6   Protection

Do not build your house on sand.

This, in a nutshell is what this chapter is about. Too many people try to build themselves up financially only to be hit with some catastrophe which totally wipes out their plans and causes real problems in their lives.

Its too easy to simply start saving or investing without protecting yourself and your family first. I absolutely believe that it is selfish and ignorant in the extreme not to make provision for yourself and your family should the worst happen. In the UK and the USA today, quality protection products are so cheap that there is no reason not to put them in place.

I believe that you must put these arrangements in place before you start building your Capital Account or Income Account.

In this chapter we will consider what you need, to protect yourself and your family. Now you may well consider that you want more protection. That's OK. What we will be looking at is the bare bones of the protection that you need. We will be taking into account any provision that you may be given with your employer, but I will not take into account state provision. I do this for two reasons:

1. Welfare rules change so frequently that as soon as we print them they are out of date.

2. A number of welfare payments are affected by definitions made by the DSS. These can vary depending on where you live and so it would be unwise to include these as they may well change from London to Luton.

I recommend that you get the help of your Independent Financial Adviser to put these arrangements in place. The Adviser will be able to source the best priced products for each area, and will consider subtle differences in policies of which you may not be aware. In this chapter you will gain sufficient information to tell the adviser what you want, they will then simply make the arrangements to put in place those plans.

Protection is broken down into three different areas: Wills, Life and Health.

Wills

I have both arranged and written over 10,000 Wills as well as dealt with countless estates following death, and with the exception of single people with estates of under £50,000, having a professionally drafted Will is one of the best investments you will make on behalf of your family.

Without a Will your estate will be subject to the laws of intestacy. This means that it is these intestacy rules that will decide who gets what in the event of your death. With a valid Will in place you can both deal with your estate efficiently, as well as nominate Guardians for your children, nominate Executors and Trustees to control the estate and mitigate a degree of Inheritance Tax. All of these things can be accomplished with a Will. So why do over 70% of the UK population not have a valid Will? It beats me!

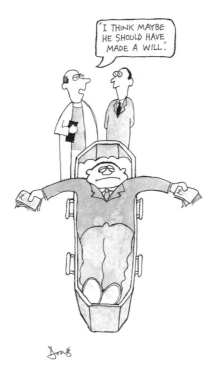

So who should draft your Will?

I firmly believe that a specialist should draft your Will. Now this may mean a specialist Will writing company, a specialist Estate Planning Solicitor, or your Financial Adviser. The important thing is to use a specialist. I have seen many Wills written by people themselves and by solicitors, who are just general practitioners, they are not only badly written, but actually make the situation in the event of their death worse rather than better. So use a specialist who not only drafts the Will to your wishes but who also gives Inheritance Tax planning advice. This will mean that you can then plan your requirements to ensure that what you want is passed down without the taxman getting his hands on it.

In drafting your Will, take special care to make provision for the education and maintenance of your children if under the age of 18. This is a point often forgotten, but with correct use of the right clause and a trust, children can be effectively provided for.

Life Insurance

It's boring, it's gloomy and it's depressing, but I can assure you that, if your family need to make a claim it is the best piece of paper that you can have.

In the modern world its good to know that the mortality rate (that is the rate at which people die) has fallen and will probably continue to fall as we live longer and longer. This has the beneficial result of reducing the cost of life insurance to very low levels. In fact the present cost of life insurance has fallen to about 50% of its costs only 20 years ago. This means that there is no reason not to have it!

Who needs it?

If you are single and have no dependants then you do not need life insurance. The only time when life cover is advisable is if your family has a history of life threatening illness, such as cancer or heart disease. If it does, it may make sense to put life cover in place now while you are fit and well and when the premiums are extremely cheap. This would give you protection now, which can be continued should you become uninsurable in the future.

Anyone who has somebody who is financially dependent upon them needs to put life insurance in place. If you were to die, and there is someone who needs your financial support, be they spouse, children, or parents for example, you need life cover.

How much do I need?

There are two amounts you need. The first is an amount to cover debt, the second is an amount to replace your income.

I firmly believe that you must cover all existing debt with both life and critical illness cover (see health section). This means that you have an amount of life insurance that covers your mortgage liabilities as well as any other borrowings that you may have. It also means that in the event of your death these debts would be 'self cancelling'. The loans would be linked to the life insurance directly to ensure that the debts were cleared in the event of your death. This would avoid the complications of probate on inheritance tax on the life cover.

There are many different opinions regarding how much life insurance a person should have to replace his income. These range from 'ten times salary' to 'twenty times salary'.

I believe, however, that the amount of life cover that you must have depends on what existing cover you have, your liabilities and your income.

In the event of your death your family will lose your income. If you want to ensure that they maintain the same standard of living then you must replace that level of income. To replace the income they will require a capital lump sum, to invest to generate an income, in exactly the same way as you will with your Financial Independence.

Let's look at an example:

If you earn £20,000 per year and you were to die, this is the level of income that would be lost. However this is not necessarily the same as the level of income required to maintain the same standard of living. If you had a mortgage and paid, say £500 per month in mortgage payments and insurance payments, then, provided that your debt is covered by life insurance only an income of £14,000 is required to maintain the same standard of living. Now, from the chapter on financial independence goals, you know how to calculate the capital amount that is required to generate this income. However, unlike previously, do not use your risk rating. As we are dealing with your families well being we cannot really take an undue risk as you will not be around to make up any shortfall, and so I suggest using a risk return of 5%.

If you need an income of £14,000, and you are generating a return of 5% then you will need a capital sum of £280,000. I.E. £280,000 invested at 5% pa will generate an income of £14,000.

From this figure you can now deduct the existing life cover that you have in place. This may include death in service benefit from your employer and other forms of life cover that you may have in place. If, for example you have a death in service benefit of £40,000 then the extra life cover that you require is £240,000.

To calculate the level of cover required complete the following calculation:

Present Level of income:	£
Less those liabilities that will be cleared in the event of death (i.e. they have the correct level of cover assigned to them, for example your mortgage)	£
Subtotal (A)	£
Divide (A) by 0.05 to give the gross amount of cover required	£
Less existing life cover	£
Subtotal (B)	£
Add (A)	£
Subtotal (C)	£

Subtotal (B) is the amount of additional life cover that you will require to produce on income equal to the income lost in the event of your death, if the capital is invested and produces a return of 5%pa. However, because interest will not be generated until the capital has been invested for twelve months you must add an additional one year's worth of required income.

This calculations assume that:

1. Your family will invest the funds received from life insurance.

2. Your family can achieve a return of 5% on the investment

What type of cover?

What type of life policy should you have? There are many types of cover available. Term, Whole of Life, Pension Term, Convertible Term, Endowments, Renewable Term, Annually Renewable, to name the most popular. The newspapers would have you believe that term cover is the only type of cover you should have. However, this view seems to stem more from the financial journalist's envy of the commissions payable to advisers than to any real understanding of the products available.

The real deciding factor is the term that you want the policy to be in place for.

If you only want the policy to last ten years then you can restrict the cover to a ten year period. If however, you need the policy to go on forever, then to have a term on the policy would not match your needs. So how do you choose?

I think that you should choose your life cover from Term, Convertible Term or Whole of Life. Each of these types has its own advantages and disadvantages, with each type matched to a different set of circumstances.

TERM COVER

This type of cover is mainly suited to the person that wants life cover in place to cover a certain event. In my experience this is usually put in place to provide protection until children are grown and fully independent. If, for example you have a child aged 5 then you may want cover in place until your child is age 21, when you may realistically expect them to be Financially Independent.

CONVERTIBLE TERM

Like term cover convertible term (CTA) provides cover for a specified period. In addition to this it provides the option to convert the policy to another type of insurance, usually Whole of Life, an Endowment or another Term policy, prior to the end of the term. Again this policy would be used to provide cover to match a specific event, but will often be chosen if it was felt that your circumstances would change over time, or if you could not afford the premium for Whole of Life cover. All else being equal I would always recommend Convertible Term over Term because of the added flexibility that it provides. Even though it is about 10%-20% more expensive it is worth the cost.

WHOLE OF LIFE

As the name suggests, Whole of Life cover provides cover for the whole of your life. This means that your family will definitely be claiming and the insurance company will definitely be paying out. Now the insurance companies do not really want to pay out the insurance and so the policy is designed to build a cash or surrender policy. This value will be paid out in the event of the policy being surrendered. In effect this is an incentive to surrender the policy and take the money and run. Most of these plans are now costed so that the surrender value will equal the premiums paid after about 12-15 years. After that date the surrender value will continue to build. Obviously the actual return of the policy will depend upon the charges to the plan and the returns of the investment into which the funds are invested.

This type of policy is often used by parents who want to provide cover while their children are growing up, but want the policy to provide a lump sum for university or a wedding for example.

The type that you will choose will depend upon two factors, the term that you require cover for and the budget that you have available. I suggest that you have your Adviser consider the costs of each type of plan so that you can chose the one that best suits your circumstances.

Using a Trust

It is vital in setting up your life policy that you use the right type of Trust for the policy. The right Trust will do two things, it will ensure that the right person receives the money at the right time without the need for gaining probate, and secondly it will help to avoid Inheritance Tax.

This is a complicated area and your should seek your advisers recommendations directly.

Health

The value of Health Insurance to an individual or family can not be over emphasised. I have seen so many families lose their homes, have their finances destroyed and their futures ruined because they have not had sufficient cover in place. I have had some clients say that they do not need this type of cover and that their family will help out if the worst happens, or that their employer is very benevolent and will understand if they must have time off work. However, I only have to recount one of the many times when I have had to foreclose on a families home because they could not meet the mortgage payments for them to realise that this is to important to be left to chance or someone else's goodwill.

Health cover comes in two main forms. Permanent Health Insurance (PHI) also known as Income Protection Insurance and Critical Illness Cover (CIC). Each is different and is designed for a different set of circumstances. In an ideal world you would have both types of cover, but often a clients budget will only provide for one type of cover. If this is the case with you then I recommend that you put PHI into place, with CIC being added as your circumstances improve. Having said that I believe you need to provide CIC cover for all debts that you may hold. This is because the cost of CIC cover, when added to life cover is relatively cheap and so can be added quite easily.

As with life cover you should use your IFA to find the best policy for you in the market place. There are many different options, with each policy having its own 'bells and whistles' and so it is important to find the right policy at the right price.

What cover should you have?

In the UK income paid from PHI is paid free of tax. The PHI policy is an income replacement policy. This means that in the event of your not being able to work due to illness, accident or injury, the policy replaces your income until you either return to work or reach the end of the policy term.

As the income is paid without liability to tax it is your net income that needs to be replaced. Unfortunately, each insurance company has its own levels of benefit that are available. Your IFA will be able to convert your gross income to the maximum level of cover that can be obtained from the relevant insurance company.

The levels of cover provided by CIC are calculated differently. CIC pays out a tax-free cash lump sum in the event of diagnosis of a defined critical illness. Defined illnesses range from heart attack to cancer, heart decease, etc. Policies usually cover 8 core illnesses with the better policies covering up to 40 illnesses.

Provided that you have CIC on your existing levels of debt then the remaining cover that I recommend to clients is two years net income. I recommend this because this is the average time that is spent off work by those recuperating from a critical illness. However, this is not a hard and fast rule and it is important that you set this level of cover to your own personal circumstances. I suggest that when setting this type of policy into place that you consult with your IFA.

Planning for the future

It is important to remember that while we are putting these policies into place they are only temporary measures. As we build your levels of capital then you can start to reduce the levels of both life and health cover. Clearly, if you are Financially Independent then, provided that your estate is set up so that your assets can pass to your family then life and health cover will not be required. As I mentioned earlier becoming seriously wealthy is an evolving process. This means that your circumstances will continue to change and so you must ensure that your plans and arrangements change in line with these circumstances.

Chapter 7 Savings

If you have worked through this book in order you will have the correct personal belief system in place, the goals that will drive you and keep you on course, and you will have put the basic requirements for Financial Protection in place. We can then move on to work at building your capital base.

You will recall from the goal setting chapter that, once you have the required levels of protection in place, we need to build a capital sum to make you Financially Independent. This means that you need a cash lump sum that, if invested, will generate sufficient income to meet your requirements.

There are various ways to build this capital sum, however, if you are like 98% of the population you will need to start by simply saving. If you already have a capital sum, we simply need to make this larger then you can move onto the section on investing, and then return to this chapter once you have made the relevant investments. If you do not have a capital sum to start with, then we need to build one, and build one quick so that you have something to work with.

Building your initial capital

There is an old saying that 'money attracts money', and you know whoever wrote that was right. It is easier to make money if you already have it and if you think about it this makes perfect sense. If you have money than you are probably the type of person who knows how to either make it, or grow it. But my guess is that if you are reading this book you are not one of those. From my experience, only those who don't have wealth want to attract it. Those that do, simply want to hold onto it and not lose it.

If you do not have any capital to start with then there are only two ways to build an initial lump sum: save or borrow.

In the chapter on accelerating your plan you will find details on using OPM (other people's money). If you read this you will see that I am not very keen on borrowing for anything other than for buying property. I strongly recommend that you do not borrow to invest and to build your capital sum. This is akin to speculation and I urge you to avoid it.

That then leaves only one option, saving.

You may recall my comments from the introduction when I said that becoming seriously wealthy was 'simple', I did not say it was 'easy', and this chapter will point this out. It sounds very easy to save money so that you can invest it and indeed it is, but if that is the case why do you not save on a regular and substantial basis now. The answer is that it is easier not to. It is far easier to spend all your money. In a 'credit' available economy like the one that we have it is easy to live beyond your means. So if it is so easy not to do the right thing how do we stop the old habitual pattern of spending and build the new habit of saving?

The answer is simple, we have already done it, all we need do now is install a plan. If you have taken the action noted in the book, and especially if you have fully worked all of the exercises in 'The Why' you will have re-wired your belief structure towards money. You will want to save money and reach Financial Independence, and you will have the willpower to carry it through. If not, then you need to work through that section again.

Now that we have an adequate level of desire, and a supportive belief structure in place, we can work on our savings plan.

Planning to save

The objective is simply to save sufficient money to build your capital. Now this means that saving, is not a short-term prospect, it is one that will continue on for as long as is required; i.e., until the required level of capital has been built. But how do we save on consistent and meaningful basis? The answer depends on your personal circumstances.

Broadly speaking there are two types of income: Fixed and Variable.

Each savings method will vary according to your income type.

Fixed: If you are on a salary or a set wage then you are on a fixed income. If you are on a fixed income then you will have the same level of income coming in to your household every week or month, with very little variation.

Variable: If your income varies by more than one or two percent then you are on a variable income. For example, you may typically be self-employed, or on a commission income. You may be employed, but a great deal of your income is made up of overtime or bonus arrangements. Typically your income will vary a great deal over a year

Fixed income plan

You will recall from earlier on that we calculated the minimum income that was required to maintain your present standard of living. In effect we calculated your basic budget. It is this that we will now work with. In 99.9% cases I find that people have more income that is required to meet their standard of living. If that's so, I can hear you say, why is it that I do not have any money, why do I have more month left at the end of the money, than money left at the end of the month?

To understand why this is the case you need to understand that there are basically two type of people in the world. Those who save first and spend the rest and those who spend first and save the rest. It is inevitable that the first group, those who save first and then spend the rest, will be wealthier than the second group. The reason is clear, if you make saving a priority then you will do it, if you don't then you won't.

It is clear then, that we need to put you in the first group and to do so you need to action the following plan.

Step one: Develop a budget

You will have developed a budget in the previous chapter, however, it is important that this is exact, and so I want you to go back and review your figures. Review the budget of outgoings that you have, ensure that everything is included. Once you have done this go through the budget and ask yourself, do I really need this expenditure, what can be done to reduce this expenditure now or in the future?

Now that you have a budget for your outgoings you can see exactly where your money goes! That's unless you're like most of the population and you notice that you have a large chunk of money that is not accounted for. Don't get upset or spend all night looking for the leak, you are probably like most of the population and cannot account for between 5% and 25% of your income. But that's OK, at least we know there is a leak and we can plug it.

Step Two: A commitment to save first

Now that you know how much money you need to live on, why not save the rest? I will tell you why not, because it won't work unless we build the savings habit over time. We must ensure that you save first. For you to do this you must understand that whatever you save you can afford to save. This is why we work through the budget in such fine detail. If you know your monthly budget is £1250 and your income is £1500 then you know that you have £250 spare, and if you know you have £250 spare then you will appreciate the fact that you can afford to save £100.

So look at your surplus, and whatever it is halve it, this will be our starting point. If your surplus is £500, then we start with £250, if your surplus is £1000 we start with £500, if it is £50 we start with £25.

Once you have found the correct amount, you must set up a direct payment method, a standing order for example, to be paid on the day your pay is received. The standing order must be paid directly into your basic savings account, i.e. your Capital Account, if this is not at the required level, or the deposit section of your Income Account. It is vital that this money is paid automatically before you pay your other bills. You must understand that you must pay yourself before you pay Mr Mortgage or Mr Telephone, and you will only do this if it is set up as a strict system automatically.

Step three: Review and increase

Now that you are saving regularly, we want the level of saving to settle at the maximum amount that you can afford. To do this you must regularly review the amount saved. As we started with only 50% of the possible saving then we have plenty of room to increase.

To do this I recommend that you review your level of saving once every three months. The important thing to remember is that you can only review upwards. This means that once you have increased the amount that you are going to save you can not decrease it. You must, therefore be certain that you can afford and keep to the increased amount.

Variable Income Plan

Most people, who have variable income, are self-employed, run their own business or are paid commission or bonus as part of their remuneration. This group will find that they can get to Financial Independence quicker than the fixed income group. However, while their savings system is no more complicated than the fixed income system, they will often find it more difficult to keep to. This is because the type of person that is attracted to this type of employment is more likely to be happy with financial instability, and so will often spend more easily, and find it harder to save increased income that they have worked so hard for. The system is, therefore, designed to take account of this type of mind set.

Step one: Develop a budget

Unfortunately, you cannot get away with not making a budget, as do those on a fixed income. This should be done in the same way as noted above. Again, I understand that it can be boring, but it is vital to establish exactly how much income you need.

Step two: Commit to a percentage of saving

As your income is variable, it is important to ensure that months when income is below that required to meet your budget are provided for from the good months. You probably already do this either consciously or unconsciously, but now we will make it more formal.

Now that you have your budget you will know how much excess

income you have in a month. From this excess you must now put aside 50% into a separate account to cover potential income shortfalls in future months. It may be that you will never have a shortfall. If that is the case then once every three months you will take 50% of the 50% provision and invest that with your ongoing savings. The other 50% will be held back as a 'bonus' (see step 3)

The remaining excess will be saved. Unlike those on a fixed income you can not predict the amount that you will save and so you must accept that some months this will be a large figure and some months it may be nothing. But, whatever the excess, once you have made your income provision, the remainder will be saved.

Step three: Keep with the plan

I have found that those people on a variable income have the ability to spend it before they get it. They will easily spend additional income without a second thought. If they find that they have earned a great deal in one month, the temptation is to want to 'reward' themselves for their hard work and spend the money. I understand this to be the case, and I also understand that if you make saving the be all and end all of your finances you will quickly get bored and will not keep to the plan. For this reason there is one additional point. Once every three months 50% of the surplus from the provision fund will be your bonus. It will be a sum that you can spend without guilt or recrimination. Because you have saved first you will find that you will feel a great deal happier spending than previously was the case. In fact, it is my experience that you will find that you do not want to spend a great deal of this bonus and will start saving a portion as the process of saving becomes habitual and addictive.

A Savings Goal

In my financial planning practice, clients will usually ask me, once they have committed to saving regularly, what should be their goal? This is a difficult figure to calculate, as everyone has a different set of circumstances. However, as a general rule of thumb, the minimum level of regular savings should be 10% of your net income. Note, this is a minimum acceptable standard, not a goal in itself. Now, if you have a very low level of income and 10% represents a larger portion of your income than you can realistically afford, then 10% must be your goal.

But, in most cases 10% can be reached very quickly, usually within the first 12 months, and so this should be your first savings goal, to save 10% of your net income.

Your target savings level will then depend on how soon you want to be Financially Independent. If you are happy to wait for 20 years to be Financially Independent then 20% of your income is a realistic goal. However, if you want to be Financially Independent within 5 years then you need to be saving over 50%. Whatever your goal, the most important thing is to work the process. This means agreeing with yourself how much you will save and sticking with the relative plan depending whether you are on a variable or fixed income.

Dealing with lump sums

What happens when you have additional unexpected lump sums? These may be an additional bonus from work, a gift or other unexpected forms of one-off income.

There is a simple rule with this type of income. Save half spend half.

Whenever you receive a single lump sum that is not budgeted for then you must put half in your savings account and spend half. By doing this your, will find two things happen. Firstly, you will feel more comfortable spending half as the saving has already been taken care of. You will not feel guilty spending that money, as your subconscious will know that you have saved first. Secondly, by taking half of the money to spend you will not resent saving the other half. If you had saved all the money then you will inevitably start to resent saving as you will feel that you are always saving for tomorrow and never benefiting today. By spending half, you will avoid this feeling and ensure that you keep on track with your saving.

Chapter 8   More Savings

So you are now saving. If you have taken the action that the last chapter described you will have set out a budget and implemented a plan to save on a regular basis. Almost everybody should have some form of saving plan, as it is important to build your capital lump sum as soon as possible. It is only once you have built this lump sum that we can begin to invest it correctly to work towards your capital requirements and ultimate Financial Independence.

However, we can only go so far by simply saving from your income. Eventually, if you are working your plan correctly, you will get to the point where you are saving the maximum that you can. After all, you only have a finite amount of income and you will have a degree of expenses, which are fixed. The difference being the amount that you can save. Once you are saving this, what can be done to increase your level of savings?

There are only two courses of action open to you to increase your level of disposable income, and thus the amount that you can save. Very simply, you can either reduce your expenses or increase your income. Now that we want to increase our savings we must look at strategies that can either reduce the amount that you are spending or alternatively increase your levels of income.

Reducing your costs

Imagine that you are a company, and that your shareholders required that you increase your levels of profitability. What would you do?

If you are like the vast majority of business owners then your first action will be to look at your outgoings, your expenses. How can these be reduced? How can we get the more benefit for each pound that we spend? How can we get the same benefit for less cost?

This is the same way that you must think. You must think of yourself as Me Ltd. As such you must be hard and aggressive in reviewing your expenses with a view to reducing them.

Now, if you have drawn up a budget, as I recommended in the last chapter, you will have an idea of your outgoings, and if you are like most people you will wonder why your budget shows that you have more cash left after you expenses than you actually do. The reason for this is that we all overspend in some area. Either we eat expensive sandwiches at work rather than make then at home and take them with us, or we buy that extra CD that we simply must have and then only listen to it once.

By reviewing our budget we can become more aware of our spending patterns and how our spending can be reduced or simply better controlled. However, we need to look more deeply to find ways to improve our levels of saving. There are many ways to reduce and better control our expenses, but unfortunately most will only produce small changes to our levels of expenditure. For example, you can buy the stores' own brand goods, rather than well known brands, but this is only going to save pennies as well as give the wrong instructions to your subconscious. I, therefore suggest only looking at the three main points of expenditure that are common to most families.

1. Mortgage Costs

In the UK upwards of 70% of the population have purchased their home through the use of a mortgage. In the USA this figure is lower at 50%. In my experience however, it is usually those people that have purchased their own homes that are the same segment of society that are keen to develop Financial Independence.

So how can we reduce your mortgage costs?

In my day to day practice as a Financial Planner I have seen thousands of clients that have mortgages, but less than 5% of these actively review their mortgage to ensure that they are getting the best deal. You see, just because you have an existing mortgage and it is for say, 25 years, does not mean that you must keep that mortgage with the same lender? What is there to stop you from moving to a new lender to obtain a better 'deal' than the one you have presently?

Lenders are continually reviewing their products in order to attract new business. In the UK the mortgage market is near saturation point. This means that the lenders can only continue to grow if they can increase market share. This means taking more business from other lenders.

What action should you take?

There are presently about 3000 different mortgage products on the UK market. This means that the chance of finding the best deal for yourself is quite unlikely. It is, therefore, important to consult your friendly IFA for advice.

Your first decision should be what type of mortgage do I want to change to. The basic options are:

- fixed rate
- discounted rate
- capped rate
- cash back

There are also various combinations of these types of mortgage but these are the basic types to choose from.

MORTGAGES

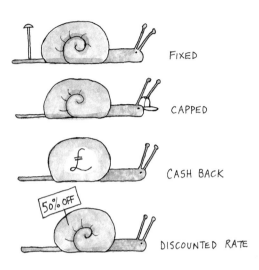

FIXED

CAPPED

CASH BACK

DISCOUNTED RATE

Dong

Fixed Rate

Fixed rate mortgages are, as the name suggests, fixed. This means that the interest rate that you are paying will be fixed for a certain period of time. This can vary from 1 year up to 10 years. With this type of mortgage there will typically be a fixed 'lock-in' period. This means that you must stay with the lender for a fixed period after the fixed period has ended. This is not always the case, however, and so I suggest looking for those deals without a 'charging' or 'lock in' period.

The time to take a fixed rate is just prior to interest rates increasing. Obviously, this is difficult to time, but it is an area that your IFA will help you with.

Discounted Rate

A discounted rate is a rate where you pay a variable interest rate, but you have a 'discount' on the rate that you are paying for an agreed period of time. For example, interest rates may be at 7% and you have a 2% discount for a two-year period. This means that you will actually pay 5% for the two-year period if rates remain the same, if rates fall to 6.5% then the rate that you are paying falls to 4.5%. Conversely, if rates increase to 7.5%, then your rate increases to 5.5%. Again, as with fixed rates, you may find that there are lock-in period with many lenders, and so it is vital that you obtain advice on the small print.

Discounted rates form the middle ground between capped and fixed. They are best when rates are falling, and there is little expectation that they will rise within the term periods. You will also find that discounted rates will usually give you a lower rate than both fixed and capped rates. This is because the lender is taking less of a risk than with the other types of rate.

Capped Rates

Capped rates are often thought of as the panacea of loan types. This is because they offer the best of both worlds. With a capped rate, you are given a ceiling to the rate that you will pay for the offer period. If during the offer period rates fall, and they fall below your ceiling rate then your interest rate payable will reduce. If, on the other hand rates increase, then you are 'capped' at the ceiling rate. Clearly this will give you great benefits, as the lender is the one that is taking all of this rate risk. For this reason you will find that the rates offered with capped loans are not usually as good as those with discounted and fixed rates.

Cash Back

Cash back loans, as the name suggests, provide you with a 'cash-back' when taking out the loan. In effect, the lender calculates the cost of offering the various discount, capped or fixed rates and averages the figure. Then rather than providing a lower interest rate, the lender gives a proportion of the calculated cost to the borrower as a single lump sum. In effect this will be an incentive to change mortgages to them. Clearly, this can have some advantages over the other types of loan, but at the same time the up front benefit will not usually be as great as the benefit over time, provided by a capped, fixed or discounted offer.

Which one should you choose?

The type of loan that you chose will depend on two different factors. Your circumstances, and the deals available to you when looking to switch lenders.

If you have not built your capital account to the required level, then there is only one choice, the cash back loan. Most cash back loans will provide between 5% and 8% as a cash lump sum. This means that, if you have the average UK mortgage of £70,000, you will receive a cash back of between £3500 and £5600. After costs of approximately £500 you will then boost your capital account by a substantial amount. In most cases this means that you can instantly achieve the goal of building a capital account!

If however, you have already built your capital account then you should really be looking to reduce your mortgage costs rather than seeking a one-off cash injection as the overall benefit of a reduced mortgage will provide you with better benefits in the long term.

So which one of the three should you choose?

The overriding point to consider, in my opinion is to only move to a lender that calculates interest on a daily or monthly basis as compared to an annual basis. (Look to the examples and reasons given in the chapter on destroying debt for more details) I believe that this is more important than any rate comparison as it massively affects the amounts that you will pay on the mortgage over time.

So you will have narrowed your choice down to only those lenders that use monthly or daily-calculated interest charges. Your choice should then be limited to those lenders that do not apply a charge or penalty to the loan, should you want to switch or settle the mortgage at the end of the offer term. While it is better than nothing, you do not really want to be tied to the lender once the offer period has finished, as you will want to look again for another offer to maintain your benefits.

So you have now narrowed the choice down to those lenders that offer a daily or monthly calculated interest rate, and that have no lock-in period at the end of the offer. Your choice will then simply be to choose the lender with the best overall deal. The best overall deal is the one that, once all the charges are taken into account, will provide the best total saving assuming that rates do not change. Unless the circumstances are very clear with regard to interest rate it is very difficult to project how they will move, and so it is probably best to ignore this point and simply go with the best over all deal.

This is where you should use your IFA. The IFA can help you identify the best provider from various software and research arrangements that they will have. In using your IFA I strongly suggest that you agree a fee for the work. This means that the IFA will not be taking any "procreation" fees into account, as you will be meeting their costs. While the costs of this service varies around the country you should expect to pay between £300 and £500.

2.. Loan Costs

Approximately 70% of the UK population have credit, in one form or another. While it is called 'credit', this is the best confidence trick in the world as it is not a credit, it is a debt! The only people to get credit are the lenders.

I have found that most people have no idea how much they are paying for their debt. They simply cannot tell if they are paying too much or have a fair agreement. In fact, most people do not even understand how to compare relevant rates and deals and so are totally ignorant of their situation.

Obviously, the best situation to be in is one where you have no debt. (With the exception of tax deductible debt.) To peruse this please review the chapter on 'Destroying Debt'. However, if you are comfortable with the levels of debt that you have then the next area to concentrate on is reducing the costs that you are paying.

The first thing to do is to find out what debt you have and the interest rates that you are paying. The interest rates you are looking for is the APR. Do not be swayed into looking at the flat rate, the annual rate or the monthly rate. Only look at the APR. The APR is the figure that takes into account all the charges that you will be charged for the transaction, taking into account the term of the loan. Once you have established the total amount of debt that you have, the remaining term and the rate that you are paying then you can take one of two courses of action.

- you can look for another loan provider to 'consolidate' your loan. This means clearing your existing higher rate loan with a single lower rate loan. Now, don't get to hung-up on the term of the new advance, it is the APR that is the most important thing. If the APR is lower than your existing loans, then so will the payment be.

- you can negotiate with you existing lender to move to a lower rate. The world of lending is a tough one and all companies have their own targets. It is usually in their best interests to agree to reduce your interest rate than to lose you as a customer. Again, if you can shave just a few points off your rate you will reduce your payments. Any reduction in payment will then allow you to increase your level of saving, or alternatively continue with the present level of payment and reduce the debt more quickly.

3. Car loans and Expenses

After your home the greatest expenditure that most families have is the expenses relating to the motor car. The car is usually the greatest single capital payment that we make after buying our own home, and the regular monthly expenses for the car (insurance, fuel, tax etc.) are usually the greatest regular expense.

Again, I could simply make a list of obvious cost reduction techniques such as finding the cheapest fuel cost, using a fuel garage with a loyalty scheme, shop around for the best price for servicing, but these will have only small effects on your budget. Now I am not suggesting that you should not do them, in fact I strongly encourage you to do all of these simple cost reduction techniques, however, in my experience, these ideas are ones that you already know and are probably doing. If you are not, it is either that you have not got the time or inclination to do them or that you are not taking financial independence seriously. Either way, I want to concentrate on ideas that will have a much greater effect I have with mortgages and loans.

So, on the assumption that you have and need a car, how can we generate real savings in its costs? Here, the real secret is to get the taxman to help. Yes, you read it correctly, get the taxman to help! This brings me onto a technique that I use with many personal clients. The technique is to simply set up a business to 'funnel expenses' and make them tax deductible. This is one of the best ways to reduce you costs.

Using a business to reduce expenses

If you are self-employed or run a small business then you will know the advantages of tax deductions on your accounts. Tax deductions are expenses that are made in the course of your business. They are expenses that are deducted from your turnover, to derive a profit figure. The greater the level of deduction the lower the level of profit, the lower the level of profit the lower the tax payable.

For example, if we assume you have a business with £10,000 of income, and the tax rate is 20% (excluding allowances for the time being) the tax payable will be £2000. If, however, you have expenses running the business, of £5,000, then the income will be £10,000 less expenses of £5,000 giving a profit of £5,000 and a tax liability of £1000. Obviously this is a simple example and does not take into account the relatively complicated UK tax system, but the process is sound.

So how can this be used in the real world?

The first thing to do is to set up a business. This can be for any purpose. However, I recommend that you consider two different areas: Hobbies and Multi-level marketing.

Hobbies

If you have a hobby why not look at making it into a business. For example, if you enjoy stamp collecting, then why not start trading in stamps. If you enjoy going on skiing holidays, why not start to organize your own skiing trips. If you like fishing, why not start up a fishing club. Virtually any hobby that you have can be turned into a business of some sort. Using a hobby as a business has two distinct advantages. Firstly, as it is your hobby you will usually enjoy the activity, and secondly, you will usually have a degree of knowledge or competence that you can bring to the business.

Multi-level Marketing

Muti-level marketing or network marketing as it is also called is a low cost way of getting into business. Unlike its predecessor, pyramid marketing which is now banned in the UK, Multi-level marketing involves running your own business, and encouraging others to also join the business. This can be an excellent way of getting into business as the set-up costs are marginal and there is a sound support system in place to help you build the business.

By setting up a business you will reap the reward of having deductible write-offs. This will both reduce your tax liability and may even generate some profit that can be invested.

An example

Lets assume that you enjoy photography, and so want to use this as a basis for your new business. So you decide to set-up a business taking photographs of the children of friends, parties, perhaps even weddings, if you are good.

In running your business in the first year you have a turnover of say £3000. Against this you write-off various expenses such as a proportion of your telephone bill, lighting and heating costs, travelling costs. These all account for say £2500. This leaves you with a profit of £500 on which we will assume the tax is 20%, equaling £100. This liability of £100 will be much less than the expenses of £2500 that you have written off, thus reducing your over all outlay.

Let us assume that you want to purchase a car and take out a car loan on which the repayment is £150, £100 of which is interest and £50 of which is capital repayment. Excluding capital write-downs this means that you have a further tax deductible expense of £1200 per year. If we assume that you have a tax liability of £4000 from your existing employment, then you can reclaim the tax paid by the amount of loss that you have made.

Therefore:

Turnover	£3000
Expenses	£2500
Interest	£1200
Net loss	£700 – This is reclaimable from the revenue!

A WORD OF WARNING

While the principles of this are very simple the practicalities can be somewhat complicated. I strongly recommend that you speak with your IFA about these arrangements and ensure that you complete them correctly. If your IFA is unable to help then you have got the wrong IFA. Remember their job is to give independent financial advice, not just to sell you policies. All good advisers will be able to help you, or at very least have an arrangement with a local accountant who will help.

Increasing income

There are many different ways to increase you income but the best way to do this will depend on whether you are self-employed or employed.

Self-employed

If you are self-employed then it is relatively easy for you to increase your income.

Generally speaking there are only three ways to increase you income.

- increase the size of each sale or transaction

- increase the regularity of each purchase or sale by your customers

- increase the number of customers or numbers of clients that you deal with

That's it. There are no other ways to increase business. Every idea that you come across will be just an extrapolation of one of these ideas.

It is not my intention in this book to spend time talking of ways to increase you business as I do not think this can be done well without taking a serious look at your business. I therefore, suggest that you consider looking at one of the various coaching services that are available. It may cost you a small amount to enroll in such a course, but in my experience your income will increase far in excess of the expense.

Employed

The simplest way to increase your income is to ask for a pay rise. I know that this may be a little simplistic, but have you tried it? If you are in a large company where you boss is not your employer, then it may be difficult for them to authorize a rise, however, if your boss is the owner of the business then they will be in a position to give an increase in salary. Now, they will not necessarily give you a rise, but you will definately not get a rise if you do not ask. After all, what have you got to lose?

Any other method of increasing your pay will probably mean a fundamental change in your employment circumstances, and so you need to consider what changes you may or may not want to make. For example, do you want to move to the sales department, where you will be paid on commission? Do you want to move into a position with bonuses payable? Could you move into management to a position with greater responsibility?

Perhaps the greatest thing to bear in mind is that working for someone is like getting heat from a fire. You cannot get heat from a fire by simply asking for heat, you must first put 'wood on the fire' before it will give you heat. This is the same for your employer. The main asset of any business is the staff. Good staff are hard to find. Excellent staff are often impossible to find. If you can prove how good you are to your employer by putting extra 'wood on the fire' you have got a much greater chance of reaping benefits yourself.

Chapter 9 Pound Cost Averaging and the Magic of Compound Interest

Despite the number of people with GCSE and 'A' levels in maths, people are remarkably ignorant about the mathematics of how money grows. Most people understand the general theory that they will earn interest from money deposited with a bank or building society, or that they will benefit from the growth of shares if they buy stock in a company, but few understand how these things will really impact on their savings and investments. However, these two areas, 'Pound Cost Averaging' (PCA) and 'Compound Interest' (CI) are two of the most simple and yet powerful tools in the development of becoming seriously wealthy.

Savings vs Investment

There are generally two different ways to increase the capital you hold. One way is to invest the money the other is to save the money.

Investing money mean the "risking" of part or all of your capital to produce a substantially better return than could be achieved by simply saving the money. Investing means putting the money in 'asset backed' investments. This means that the money that you invest is put into investments that you hope will grow in value and can then sell at a higher price.

Buying a house is an investment. Now, you may never actually sell the house and realize the investment, but the process of simply buying a house is investing. You are putting your money into an asset, in this case bricks and mortar, with the hope that its value will increase over time. Buying shares, investment trusts, unit trusts or OEICS is investing. Here you buy a small part of a company, or hope that the company or trust will increase in value, and so your investment will grow.

The main point to remember with investments is that there is no security of capital. Of course there are various investment products that claim to give security, but these are usually hybrids of investments and savings vehicles. Investing means taking a risk, however small. Because there is a risk associated to the investment then the value of your capital may fall as well as rise. It is this risk and movement in the value of capital that we will want to use to our advantage in Pound Cost Averaging, as you will see below.

Saving, is the process of 'lending' your money to an established financial institution. The institution will then pay you interest for borrowing that money from you. If you lend, or 'deposit' that money with them for a set period of time you will usually obtain a higher rate of return, as you will forgo the ability to obtain access to the money. If you deposit the money so that you have access to it then you will receive a lower return simply because the institution will not be able to use that money as freely, as they know you may want it back at some unknown point in the future. The point to consider with savings is that the money that you deposit has a capital guarantee. This means that the bank or building society that you are depositing the money with will guarantee that you cannot lose your capital, nor any interest that they add to that capital. Of course, this guarantee is only as strong as the institution guaranteeing it. You may recall in the late 1980's that a number of smaller institutions went out of business, the most prominent of which was BCCI. More recently problems with Equitable Life have demonstrated that even large previously well respected institutions can have financial problems that can affect customers. Fortunately, in the UK we have some investor protection. This means that the part of your capital that is deposited will be protected, but not all of it. It is for this reason that you should not hold all of your funds with just one institution, but limit yourself to a maximum of £20,000 in any one bank or building society. This will mean that you will retain the highest levels of protection that is available.

Compound Interest

Einstein commented that compound interest was the greatest secret ever kept. He understood the importance of this simple but extremely powerful financial tool. Unfortunately, many people are unaware of its ability to help them reach Financial Independence.

So what is compound interest, how does it work, and more importantly, how can it help you?

The first thing to remember is that compound interest is only generated by savings, not by investments. Interest is only generated when you place money in a deposit taking institution. When money is deposited with these deposit-taking institutions, you will receive a rate of interest. This interest is paid based on the levels of capital that you deposit. The important thing, however, is that when interest is paid, it can compound on itself. This simply means that you can earn interest on your interest, which will in return earn interest and so on. It is this process that you must use to your benefit.

The simple chart overleaf shows how a small saving of £1000 can grow over a period of time. As you can see the effects are not very great in the short term, however, over the long term the results can be enormous.

The Value of £1000 invested over 30 years at 6% interest

Number of years	Capital & Interest	Number of years	Capital & Interest	Number of years	Capital & Interest
1	£1060	11	£1898	21	£3399
2	£1123	12	£2012	22	£3603
3	£1191	13	£2132	23	£3819
4	£1262	14	£2260	24	£4048
5	£1338	15	£2396	25	£4290
6	£1418	16	£2540	26	£4548
7	£1503	17	£2692	27	£4821
8	£1593	18	£2854	28	£5110
9	£1689	19	£3025	29	£5417
10	£1790	20	£3207	30	£5742

Of course, the return that you will receive will vary based on three factors:

1. The amount that you save, and whether you increase the amount saved

2. The rate of interest received

3. The compounding term.

The amount you save may be a single lump sum investment or it may be a regular monthly amount. Clearly the more you save the more you earn, however, it is important to remember that the more you save the greater rate of interest that you may be able to obtain. Most bank or building societies will provide greater levels of interest with a greater amount put on deposit.

You can see from any local high street bank that the rate of return can increase considerably as the amount saved increases.

The rate of interest will have the most marked effect on the growth that you will receive. You can see the difference from the following chart, the massive differences that only a few percent can make. You can see clearly that the longer the money is held the greater the effect is.

£1000 saved, with no further contributions

Years saved	5% Return	7.5% Return	10% Return
5 Years	£1276	£1435	£1610
10 Years	£1628	£2061	£2593
20 Years	£2653	£4243	£6727
40 Years	£7039	£18046	£45259

The compounding term also has a great effect. The compounding term is the regularity with which the interest is added to the initial capital. In the UK most banks and building societies will add interest once every year, or in some cases once every six months. This means that your money would have to remain on deposit for either a year or six months before any interest was added, and could in turn add interest. It is better to have a short compound period. Because of the greater competition you can find many accounts that have interest added daily or monthly. In the early days this does not appear to have much effect, but in the longer term the effects can be marked.

So what does all this information about compound interest mean? How can you use it to boost your wealth?

I suggest the following strategies:

- Always use your IFA to shop around for the best interest rate. There are thousands of options on the market, and it is unlikely that, on your own, you will be able to find the best rate.

- Always look for a daily-calculated rate. This will have a tremendous impact over the long term

- If you have a very low risk tolerance to investment risk then be prepared to save for the long term. If you can use more sophisticated products such as 'with-profits bonds', and 'offshore accounts', then you can still achieve Financial Independence but it will take longer than if you were prepared to take some risk, but it is still achievable.

If you are prepared to take some investment risk then you can look at other techniques for improving your returns, such as 'Pound Cost Averaging'.

Pound Cost Averaging (PCA)

PCA, or in the USA, DCA (Dollar Cost Averaging) is a simple process which happens when you invest in asset backed investments on a regular basis over time. It is one of the reasons why regular monthly savings should be made, no matter what your existing portfolio. PCA actually allows you to benefit from falls in the level of your investment.

Take a look at the following graph:

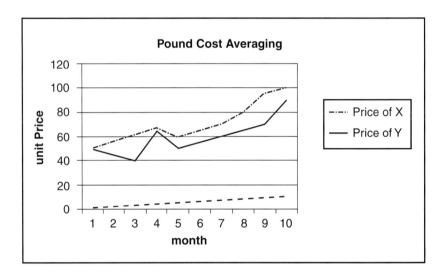

You can see that there are two lines, each representing a different share or unit price. This can be the price of a share or stock in a company, or it can be the value of a unit in a unit trust, either way the principal is still the same.

You can see that over the term of the investment you would have purchased on 10 separate occasions. During that time you could have purchased in either product X or product Y. The investment in either would have been the same. In the chart X is worth £100 at the end of the term and Y is worth just £90 at the end of the term. Based on this information you would probably choose to buy X as the value is greater at the end of the term.

However, this does not tell the true story.

Based on the price movements in each you would have purchased the following number of units:

Months	Price of X	Number purchased	Price of Y	Number purchased
1	50	6	50	6
2	55	5.5	45	6.7
3	60	5	40	7.5
4	67	4.5	65	4.6
5	60	50	50	6
6	65	4.6	55	5.5
7	70	4.3	60	5
8	80	3.8	65	4.6
9	95	3.2	70	4.3
10	100	3.3	90	3.3

If you had purchased units in X, you would own 44.7 units. At a valuation of £100 that is a **total value of £4474**. If you had purchased units in Y you would have purchased 53.5 units. With a price of £90, **your holding in Y would be worth £4812**.

You can see from this example that movement in the value of an asset is more important than the ultimate value, if you are buying it on a regular basis. This is the essence of PCA, the power of purchasing assets at a low price. In this way you will positively benefit from a fall in an assets price. Obviously, this will not help if the value of the asset never recovers, and this is why your choice of investment is so important.

Although this example is only small, the principal is sound no matter how much the size of your investment.

So how can you use this principle to benefit your Financial Plan?

The important thing to remember is that the investment is an investment, not savings. This means that your capital is at risk. For this reason it is important that you match any investment with your view towards risk and reward, as previously discussed.

I believe that there are very few circumstances where any type of investment should be made unless you have sufficient funds in your

Capital Account. Until you have a fully funded Capital Account you should not place any risk on your capital however small. However, once you have funded your Capital Account then you should consider a regular premium investment that can take advantage of PCA. Your regular investment into this, will be part of your Income Account, but also can then go on to be part of your total capital towards Financial Independence.

There are many schemes on the market that can be used for investment that will produce PCA. The type that you choose will depend on your own personal circumstances. Please ensure that you consult with your adviser to find the right type for you.

Doug

What is investing?

I am often surprised at people's confusion over investing. Many people seem to think that placing money on deposit is an investment. They think that if they place money with their local bank or building society that they will grow their money, which on one level they will. However, what they will not do is grow their money in real terms, and it is this real growth that sets aside investing from saving.

Investing is using your money to generate growth in real terms, which means growing your money in excess of inflation. Unless your money can grow in excess of inflation what is the point in saving it?

Investing means risking your capital. It means accepting that to get a greater return on your money, you must put it at risk to a degree, however small, and this is the main point most people never really understand risk and how it affects them and until they can fully understand this they are unlikely to be a successful investor.

If you have completed this book in order, you will have completed the Risk/Return section, which will point you in the general direction of the levels of risk that you may accept. However, I know, from many years of dealing with my clients, that although you may think you are a 5, 6 or 7 rating, when an investment falls you suddenly feel very uncomfortable and your desired rating falls to 3 or lower. The only way to combat this is to fully understand how investments work and why they rise and fall. You can then build this into your view of investment risk and reward and decide on a specific investment strategy.

In this chapter I will consider how an investment works and why investments can have such large gains and falls for no obvious reason. I will look at the various types of investment and ways to compare them so that you will be in a position to take the right action at the right time.

As you are putting together your financial plan, you will only begin to look at investments once you have built your Capital Fund. Until you have done this you should not look to make any investments. Too many people try to make great gains without building the proper levels of security behind them. Once you have built your Capital Account you will then have funds that you can look to invest in. To do this you must have the correct knowledge, either to set up investments yourself, or to use other people in the right way to arrange your investments for you.

How do Investments work?

The investments that I am referring to here are asset backed investments. These are investments that are actually backed by a specific asset, which will denote its value. For example, land is an asset-backed investment. The value of the asset is based on the value that we put on the land, which in turn is valued by the demand for land. Shares in companies are also asset-backed investments. With shares or equities as they are sometimes called, you own a small piece of the issuing company. You own a share in the company, hence the word share.

So how does the value of your investment fall and rise and what is the real underlying value of the asset?

The thing to understand about investments is that they are only worth what someone else is prepared to pay for them. This does not necessarily mean that this is a fair or true price and does not necessarily mean that the value of the underlying asset is worth what people are prepared to pay for it, which is a strange thing, but that is the way investments work.

To understand this better let's look at an example and let's look at shares in a company, as this is an easy thing to relate to.

Consider ABC Bank PLC. ABC Bank PLC is a profitable business, which has many branches and is well thought of in the world of finance. The company is 'worth' in its accountant's eyes £1,000,000. (Obviously this is a very small bank, but it makes the figures easier to understand!) When it started trading it issued 500,000 shares. This means that each share is worth in real terms £2, so, if the bank were to close down and sell everything, that it would generate a total of £1,000,000 which would be divided equally between its shareholders, each one receiving £2 each.

As the years go by, trading improves and the value of the company improves because it generates more profits, buys more assets etc. and so in a few years is valued at £2,000,000. This means that each share is now worth £4. (£2,000,000 divided by 500,000 shares).

Now, let's assume that the shares are placed on the stock market. The stock market is simply a market place where you can buy and sell shares freely. You decide that you would like to sell your small share holding and receive £4 per share. However, when you go to sell the shares you find that each share is now worth £5! But how can this be, if the company is only worth £2,000,000?

The answer is that market demand has driven up the price. It turns out, when you look into the matter, that the company has announced that it is about to buy a small bank, which is likely to make it even more profitable. Shareholders would receive a larger dividend and the real value would increase as profits are retained and re-invested into the bank. The market thinks that prospects for the company are good and so there is an increased demand for the shares. As the demand increases so does the price, simple supply and demand! In real terms the value of the company has not really changed, it is just that the market expectation of the company has increased, making its shares more in demand.

The bank buys out the new bank and the shares are now worth £6 each because of the previous increased demand. The share price remains almost unchanged over the next twelve months. However, things are not always what they seem. After profits are announced they have increased by 10%. Fantastic news you think, the share price is bound to increase and so you check the price of the shares and find out that they have fallen to £4.50. How can this be so when the company has increased its profit over the previous year?

The point to consider here is demand again. In the previous year the price of the shares increased, as there were expectations of increased profits in the future. However, although profits have increased they have not increased to the levels that were expected and so people have begun to sell shares in disappointment. This increased supply has driven down the price, despite the increase in profit and real increase in the value of the company.

This is the real point about investing. It all depends on the price that others are willing to pay for the asset, be it shares, property, gold or paintings. The simple rules of supply and demand apply.

So how does this help you when your investments fall and how can it help you not to get overexcited when they grow?

I recommend to my clients that they think of the marketplace (this can be for shares, property or any other tradeable asset) as a single man. This one man's job is to buy and sell. Some days he is happy some days sad, occasionally he is ecstatic, but often depressed! The price that he will buy and sell at will often have little or nothing to do with the true value of the asset you are holding. He will buy and sell simply based on his attitude at the time. Therefore, one day he will wake up, the sun is shining and all is fantastic. He will be very positive about business and how the economy is growing. He therefore thinks that whatever he buys is likely to increase in value and become more valuable, regardless.

And so he buys at a higher price because he wants to increase his asset holding, so that the value of that asset will increase. The next day, however, he wakes up, stubs his foot on the bed and finds that the cat has been run over by his wife who has just walked out on him because he was so unbearably happy the day before! This puts him in a foul mood and so that day he decides to sell his investments because things are bad and are going to get worse, therefore he might as well keep the cash in the bank account, no sense in risking his money. This means that by selling he will increase the number of assets available and of this increase in assets will have the effect of driving the price down.

This is simply how investments work. This price has little relationship to their value. However, the price is the realizable money that is available when you sell an asset, and here we come to the major thing to consider with an investment. Everything hinges on the time period that you hold an asset. Consider for example, in the case of ABC Bank, the fluctuation in the price only affects you if you are buying or selling. If you are simply holding the investment it does not really matter how it's price moves on a day to day basis. The 'Man' that is the market can be as fickle as he wants to be, but unless you are selling the asset it does not affect you. The important point is that the value of the asset is sound and as such will build over the course of time. If the decision to buy the asset was based on sound decisions and on accurate information it is very unlikely that you will pick an out and out turkey, although this does happen to everyone from time to time, hence you must use a sound asset allocation strategy as noted later in this chapter.

What we are attempting to achieve with an investment is consistent above average growth in the value of the investment. We are not looking for massive instant high-risk gains, this is covered in the chapter entitled "How to accelerate your plan", we are looking to build a sound financial base for our investments using a systematic investment strategy. With the correct strategy, we can build towards Financial Independence and make ourselves seriously rich even on our salaries.

Types of investment

Have you ever considered how many makes of car there on the road? There are Fords, VW's, BMW's, Rovers, Jeeps – this list goes on and on. However, the fundamental concept is the same. Each car is designed to take you, in varying degrees of comfort from point A to point B. That's it! That's all a car does and yet there are so many different manufacturers and models that it would probably be impossible to catalog all of them.

This is the same with investments. There are literally hundreds of different types, from the obvious Property, Company Shares and Government Bonds through to Unit Trusts, OEIC's, Pensions, SIPPS, Investment Trusts, Venture Capital Trusts, Business Enterprise Schemes etc. Like the car, they all have a similar theme. You want to invest capital and have the value of that capital increase over a period of time. That's all that you want an investment to do. Of course you may want to generate income from your capital, but this is simply another form of growth that is taxed differently from capital growth, and so we can ignore this for the time being.

If there are so many forms of investment and ways to invest where do we start?

Which should we use? And what's all this asset allocation stuff?

There are fundamentally three types of investment. All investments you come across are simple variations on the basic three:

• Property

• Stocks and Shares (Equities)

• Bonds

Each of the three has its advantages and disadvantages and has its place in an investment portfolio. The skill is choosing the correct mix based upon your tolerance to risk. Once you have done this you can then decide which way you would like to invest using that type of investment.

Property

All of us are aware of property. In the investment sense I refer to land you can purchase, irrespective of whether there are properties on the land.

On a scale of one to ten, property is around a 6 with regard to the level of risk that it attracts. Most people believe that property is a low risk asset, however, unless you are using a collective investment such as a Property Unit Trust, your levels of risk are relatively high. This is for two main reasons. Firstly, when people buy property, they are usually buying only one property. This means that they are putting all their eggs in one basket. They are relying solely on this one asset to make their return. It is fairly obvious, that in doing this, you are opening yourself up to many risks. For example, the property may be damaged, if you are renting it out, you may have problems finding a tenant, and you may have problems obtaining rent from them. You will be subject to the effects of both the property prices local to the property, and the local economy. For example, when IBC a large employer in the Luton area closed, many people were made redundant. This had the effect of reducing the number of purchasers on the property market as well as increasing the numbers of properties for sale. This damaged the local property market and caused the value of property to stagnate, and in a great number of cases fall, when the rest of the country was still experiencing a price boom.

The second risk that you have is that you are tying up your capital to a relatively inaccessible investment. If you should need the funds for any reason, then you must sell the property. This may take several months to complete, and once the costs have been deducted you may find that the growth in the value of the property has not been so dramatic.

I believe, however, that there is a place for purchasing property as part of an investment portfolio. I believe that purchasing property should be considered in two cases.

1. To purchase your main residence

2. To accelerate you Financial Plan

I believe that everyone has the right to own their own home. This must be one of the most important areas of Financial Independence. Once you own your own home (this means with no mortgage liability) then you are well on the way to Financial Independence. This area will be covered in detail in Chapter 13.

Secondly, I believe that it is sensible to broaden your investment portfolio to include property once you have built approximately, 25% of your capital fund for independence. You can then purchase property in the way that I describe in the chapter on accelerating you plan. Once you have 25% of your income fund then you can accept the extra risk that this will involve.

Shares, Stocks and Equities

This is probably the most widely used and well know type of investment. When people talk of investments it is usually stocks and shares that they are referring to.

Stocks and shares are the same thing. In the USA they refer to stocks and in Europe we refer to shares. Equities, are stocks and shares, and is just another generic name.

So how and when should we use equities in are investment portfolio? How can they help and what part do they form?

The first thing to consider is when do we use them in our Financial Plan? We can then move on to the different ways to use equities and how we should use other forms of investments that have equities as a fundamental part.

I strongly believe, as I have said before, that we should not invest until we have built our Capital Account. This point is so important that I will continue to repeat it. We should not take any risk at all with our assets until we have built that basic emergency fund. Once this is built then we can invest more effectively as we should not need to withdraw assets at a time when they may not be performing well. If however, you were investing with your capital account you would find that you may have to withdraw funds at the bottom of an economic cycle and would thus lose money. You should, therefore only invest once you have the Capital Account. You can then look to invest on a realistic basis and will be able to accept the various risks that investing will attract.

The Income Account consists of funds that you can invest. You can invest them in whichever way you feel most comfortable. This will obviously depend on your view towards risk and reward, and so will mean that the type of investment will vary from person to person.

As a general rule direct investment into equities will be rated at a level 7 or higher on the 1 to 10 scale of investment risk. If you are below this level you should not look to invest directly into equities, at least until you have a spread of other investments which have a lower level of risk (i.e. collective investments such as Unit Trusts, OEIC's etc, as noted below). However, if you rate yourself at 7 or more, or have a broad spread of collective investments, how do you invest in equities and which ones should you choose?

Another point to consider is time. If you are going to purchase shares, then you must accept that it is going to use up some of your time. Now, the time spent will vary depending on the strategy that you select, but at very least you will need to spend 2 hours per month, but this can rise to an hour a day. If you feel that you do not have the time, or if you know that you will end up not putting in all the time that buying stocks requires, then you should only look at investing in collective investments.

If you are going to invest in equities, I believe that you should invest directly, yourself. I do not believe in using a stockbroker's advisors service, as I feel that the costs involved in this are relatively high. For that reason I believe that you should use an execution only service. The term 'execution only', means that you decide which stock is to be purchased and give instructions to the broker to purchase them on your behalf. In this way you will only pay the broking fee and stamp duty.

I recommend using a telephone or internet facility. These are very popular and can be used easily and quickly. Simply look up the details in one of the quality daily papers or simply search under 'stock broking' on the NET.

Once you have found a broker you will open an account and deposit funds with them. You will then use these funds to purchase stock directly. As a general rule I suggest buying no less than £3000 of each stock. Any less then you will find that you pay a higher proportional broking charge.

Which stock should I buy and how long should I hold it?

There are generally two different strategies to buying stock. Each has it's place in a portfolio. The strategies are Buy and Hold and Churning.

Buy and hold

As the name suggest is this technique involves purchasing stock and holding it, in some cases for ever. This technique, while not the fastest way to build your portfolio, is extremely effective over the long term and can provide a lower risk profile than Churning. It also has the benefits of not requiring a great deal of time. You can probably spend less than an hour per week using this system as once you have selected the stock, you will then hold on to it. You will not generally need to continually track it and set a sale strategy and so this will not take a massive amount of time. The technique centres on the stock selection. It uses the same stock selection principals that Churning does, as noted below.

When buying and holding stock you simply decide on the stock to purchase, through use of the criteria noted below and purchase it. You should then nominate to have dividends to be re-invested in more stock, as you do not, at this stage, need income. You simply hold the stock until you require income. You would then look to move to bonds, which generate income. It sounds simple and it is, provided that you choose the correct companies you will find that holding the stock will produce an average return of between 6-12% per year. A good return for the time spent.

Churning

Churning is the technique of buying and selling a stock over a period of time in the anticipation that you buy it at a low price and sell it at a high price. Of course, this is what everyone is trying to do, and so you must ensure that you have a sound strategy in place to pick your stock.

Churning will take time. You cannot expect to buy and sell and get a great return without doing some work. If you intend to work this area correctly, you need to set aside a minimum of 30 minutes per day, with perhaps an hour or two at the weekend. You will need access to a regularly updated source of share prices, or a broker that will take timed sale instructions.

When churning it is best to look at Blue-Chipped Stock. A Blue-Chipped Stock is a major company. Typically it is a company that is listed in the FTSE 100, i.e. one of the largest 100 companies in the UK. This will mean that you will look to reduce your general levels of risk when Churning, as even if you pick a 'bad stock', it is unlikely to stay bad forever.

When Churning, you must first find a minimum of ten companies, as noted below. You must then track the value of their stock each day for a minimum of one month, but preferably, three. This will give you a feeling for the general price movement of each stock. You will then notice that each stock moves up and down within a set price range. On

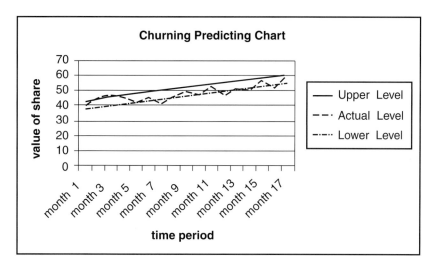

the whole you will see that the movement is upwards but does have several 'zigs and zags' within that movement.

For example:

You can see from the price movement that there is an average high and an average low. It is then relatively simple to plot a future minimum and maximum. Now, you must understand that this is the theory and that the real world can sometimes be a little different. However, by choosing the correct stock, you will be limiting your risk and ensuring that you buy a stock that has a relatively predictable future Churning price.

So how do you select stock?

In picking stock to purchase I have developed an excellent system over the last 5 years that works very successfully. The system has been built up by researching many different stock selection methods and finding the areas of similarity between them. Once this was done I used the system over a two year period, to ensure it worked and was practical. The system does not rely on tips, or looking at the market in minute detail, but simply looks to the intrinsic value of the company that you are buying part of. It uses the philosophy that suggests that you are buying part of a real company. No matter how the stock moves, you must understand that company, and it's history. If you know this, then you can forecast the likelihood of future growth. The system is specifically designed to reduce the downside of investing. It will not let you invest in the next best 'tip', or company launches, it will only let you invest in companies that are more likely to grow and improve their profit than not. That is not to say that the system is perfect. Over the past two years, I have purchased one or two poor stocks, however, this has only happened when I have not correctly analyzed a company, and gone outside the systems parameters. The system relies on being able to obtain accounting information on the company that you intend to purchase. This can be done, by contacting the company directly for a copy of the last five years accounts, or obtaining them from Companies House. Alternatively, you can purchase 'Company Refs' from HS Publishing. This is a directory of each company that produces, on one sheet, a five-year summary of the company's performance.

The Stock Selection System

To review a company, you must look at the following areas:

- 5 year growth in turnover

- 5 year growth in profit

- Growth in earnings

- Company Gearing

- Company creditors

- Cash flow

Each of the above areas must be positive, otherwise, the stock should not be purchased. As soon as you purchase a stock outside of these areas then you will increase the risk of loss without necessarily increasing the chance of gain. The rules are listed in the order of importance which means that if you are going to ignore any of the rules, then you should look to ignore the last first.

Company Gearing

Gearing is generally the degree of debt that a company has. It stands to reason that a company with more debt is more risky than one without debt. If a company has debt then less of it's income can be used to reinvest, or can be used to distribute as profit. If a company has debt then it will be affected if interest rates move up, this can have a dramatic effect on a company's profitability. The only exception to this rule is in the case of property companies. By the very nature of their business, property companies will have a great deal of borrowings. However, I suggest that rather than investing in this type of company you either make this type of investment directly, as I show in the chapter on Accelerating Your Plan, or buy investing in a property fund in a collective investment.

The maximum level of gearing that is acceptable is 30%. This means that the company must have no more that 30% of its value as a percentage of loans. Any more than this is a very big 'red light' and in my experience, if you only use one rule this is the one to use.

Sales Growth

Companies only make money when they sell something. If a company's sales are decreasing then it is unlikely that they will increase profit in the future. While sales growth on its own does not guarantee profit it is an excellent indicator of the future profitability of the company and its general direction. Very rarely, has a company that has continued to increase sales year on year experienced training difficulties, especially if its gearing is below 30%.

You should ensure two points when looking at sales:

1. There should be uninterrupted sales growth over the last five years. If there is a year where there has been no sales growth, then you must know and understand the reason for it. The reason must make sense, and point to future improvements. For example, the sales force may have been 'off the road' while training on a new product. This would lead to less immediate sales but more in the future.

2. Growth over the five-year period must be 100%. This means that sales (turnover in some companies) must be at least twice what they were five years ago. If a company has not doubled in size in the past five years you must ask yourself, if it is the type of company that is really going anywhere?

Earnings Growth

Earnings growth is the net profit that the company has made. This, as they say, is the bottom line. Unless the company is making profits it will not continue in the long term. It is important that this growth is also increasing, and so has the same two conditions as turnover:

1. Net profit must have increased every year over the last five years. There may be one exception, but the reasons for this must be known and understood and seem reasonable.

2. Net profit must be 100% greater then five years ago. As with

turnover, the net profit must be double the level of five years ago. If the company is not greatly increasing its profit then it is unlikely that people will want to buy its shares, and so increase its share price.

Return on Equity

Return on equity, is the percentage of profit that the company returns to the shareholders. Unless a company is paying a dividend then people will not buy it in the long term. As a rule return on equity must be over 10%, and have had a positive trend over the previous five years.

Creditors

Creditors can have a massive effect on a company. If its creditors demand their money, then it can have a damaging effect on a company's cash flow. For this reason it is important that the company does not have excessive creditors. To analyse this, accountants have drawn up a ratio known as the Quick Ratio. It measures the creditors as proportions of accessible assets. Only purchase stock in a company where the quick ratio must be more than one.

Cash Flow

While important, this is less so with larger companies. For this reason this rule is only to be used with small companies, i.e. those that are listed as FTSE fledglings. This rule ensures that cash flow is greater than earnings per share. Otherwise, it would demonstrate the company is not re-investing sufficiently and is drawing on capital rather than income to generate returns for the shareholders. The rule states that cash flow must be greater than earnings per share.

Whether you intend to use, buy and hold or churning, you should use the above criteria in purchasing all stock. In doing so, you will reduce the risk that you may experience and on the whole you will find that the system will produce these results:

If you were to purchase five shares:

- You would lose money on one
- You would break even on another
- You would make good return on two
- You would make an outstanding return on the other

I have tracked results over the last five years and have found the above happens on a consistent basis.

If you understand that this is how your portfolio is likely to move, then you are less likely to become upset when you lose money on one of your holdings. It is because of the fact that you will definitely lose money on one of your chosen stocks at some point, I recommend to clients that to invest in equities directly you need two things:

- Time
- Sufficient capital

Time

It will take a great deal of time if you are investing properly. At the very least you must spend two hours per week reviewing your portfolio. It takes time to find the right companies to invest in, it takes even longer to fully investigate them and then track them on an ongoing basis. If you are going to do the job properly, then you must allocate at least 30 minutes per day. Ideally this will be an hour per day, split into two sections. This way you will be able to monitor your portfolio throughout the day and make corrections as you go. This is real money that you are playing with, and so you cannot afford to become blasé and take unnecessary risks.

Sufficient Capital

To invest in equities directly, you need sufficient capital to make a spread of investments. This means that you need a minimum of £20,000, ideally £50,000. Now, of course you can invest any amount from £500 upwards, but unless you have sufficient capital then you will not be able to invest intelligently. You will not be able to produce a mix or spread of investments. You will be limited to one or two stocks, which will greatly increase the levels of risk that you are taking. This is not to say that you should not invest directly in shares unless you have sufficient capital, but that in doing so you must understand the risks that you are taking. In effect, the purchase of a single stock, if it is a blue chip company (one that is in the FTSE 100) then puts you up to an 8 on the risk scale. If you invest in a smaller company, perhaps a penny stock or a new stock, then you will increase this to a 9. So if you understand this, and build this into you plan, then there is nothing to stop you. What you must not do is to take the money from your Capital or Income Account and use it to buy what seems like a hot tip to make a killing, because it won't work. Remember if you receive a tip from someone, you are the last one on the list, everyone who buys and sells stocks for a living knows about it first and will take advantage of the 'suckers' who buy in late, and cause the stock to rise so that they can take their profit.

Bonds

Bonds are, in effect, loans. They are loans to either the Government or companies. Every Government or company has cashflow problems. They receive money at various different times. Take for example how tax is paid in the UK. Anyone who receives a self-assessment tax form will make payments on the 31st of January each year, sometimes with a follow-up payment in July. This means that while the Government is paying out throughout the year it is only receiving a large chunk of its money at two separate times.

To help with this the Government borrows to cover the cashflow. It does this in various different ways, but the most common is with the issue of Government Bonds. Government Bonds come in many different forms. Usually, they will be as Gilt Edged stock or as National Savings. For the purposes of building capital towards Financial Independence, I will exclude National Savings, as the returns generated are too small to be of any real use, unless you are using National Savings Products to hold your Capital Account. Gilt Edge Stock or Gilts as they have become know, are loans to the Government directly. With a Gilt the Government will make an 'issue'. This means that they will agree to release a certain amount of Gilts to raise a specific amount a funds to cover their expected expenditure. Each of these Gilts will have a specified life span and will pay a specified level of interest, known as a Coupon. For example, a Gilt may be issued for 9% with a 20-year life span. This means that you can buy the Gilt, often in £10,000 lots, and you will then be entitled to £900 for every £10,000 invested each year until maturity, at which time you will get back your original £10,000 invested.

Looking at it, it looks like a deposit based savings product, not an investment. However, this is where Bonds, in this case Gilts differ from savings, as they are tradable. This means that they can be traded on the open market. For example, say you hold a Gilt that pays a 9% return with 5 years to maturity, and you paid £10,000 for it, you can go to the market and sell it for the going price. This price will be based both on the price paid and the coupon (rate of interest). So, if the pervading interest rates were, say 5%, then your 9% Gilt would be worth more to a purchaser than buying a new Gilt from the Government, This means that you may receive £12,000 for your Gilt rather than the £10,000 that you paid.

You can see that buying Gilts, unless you want to purchase them simply for income, will be a similar process as with other investments as the value of them can fall and rise, depending on the levels of the prevailing interest rates. It is true that you will always receive the original face amount on maturity, but if you paid £12,000 for a £10,000 Gilt then you will make a £2000 loss. The principles are very similar to the purchase of stocks.

I do not recommend to clients that they invest directly in bonds for three reasons. Firstly, you need a large stake just to buy a bond, as the typical minimum is usually £10,000, but can be much larger. Secondly, there is very little research that can be done to develop a purchasing strategy for bonds, as you are really gambling on the future movements in interest rates, something that no one knows. Lastly, bonds have historically produced a return that is less than equities.

I therefore recommend that you only look to invest in bonds if you can use a collective, or pooled arrangement.

Collective Investments

For the majority of investors, using a collective or pooled investment is the most sensible investment strategy.

A collective investment is any investment where a number of investors pool their funds together to obtain economies of scale. This means that if 100 investors get together and invest £1,000 each they would be investing £100,000 and would be likely to obtain better 'deals' than each investing £1000. You can see that, even if they were only buying stocks, they would be able to obtain a much lower brokers charge as the broker would only do the job once rather than 100 times.

Collective investments at their most simplistic begin with Investment Clubs and move on to OEICS and Investment Trusts. The type that you choose will depend on your circumstances.

The following is a general summary of the types of collective arrangement available.

Investment Clubs

Investment Clubs are simply groups of individuals who get together to buy and sell stocks. In the UK you can have up to 20 members of an Investment Club and as few as 2 members. Typically, members will agree to contribute a single lump sum and/or a regular monthly amount to the clubs funds, which the club will then invest, based upon the agreed strategy within the club. This may mean a simple 'let's buy the football clubs' to an historical investment strategy process.

If you want to form your own club, or join an existing club I suggest that you contact Proshare, which is the London Stock Markets' own advice service for Share Clubs.

Proshare can be contacted at:

Library Chambers
13-14 Basinghall Street
London EC2V 5BQ

Information is available free and a manual on how to set up a club is available for about £30.

Unit Trusts

Unit Trusts are perhaps the most common and easy collective investments to understand, and this is perhaps why they are the most commonly used and popular in the UK. Unit Trusts are similar to Mutual Funds in the United States and are the pooled funds of many hundreds of investors, which are invested in various different asset backed investments. An investor will buy 'units' in a Trust which will form his stake in the fund. His funds are then used to buy the selected stocks and as the value of the stocks increases, the value of each of his units increases. If the stocks purchased pay a dividend, this is used to allocate additional units to the investors, thus giving him two forms of growth, the growth in the value of the unit and the increase in his share holding.

There are over 1700 different Unit Trusts in the UK covering many different types of investment. You can select a Trust that meets your exact requirements based on levels of risk, cost and investment area.

Open-ended Investment Companies (OEICS)

These are very similar to Unit Trusts, but differ in that the way they are priced is more simple. This makes their charges more transparent. There were originally designed to provide access to a Unit Trust type investment to Europe, but are becoming more popular in the UK. Many Unit Trusts in the UK are now converting to become OEICs

Investment Trusts

Despite its name, an Investment Trust is not a Trust, it is a company. However, it is a company that operates under a trust deed and exists purely for the purpose of investing. With an Investment Trust the investor will buy shares in the company, as you would do with a normal stock. Your funds will then be used to purchase shares in many other companies, in the same way that a Unit Trust would. The major difference with a Unit Trust, is that the Investment Trust can borrow money to buy additional investments. This is known as gearing, and means that an investment into an Investment Trust will usually attract more risk than the equivalent Unit Trust.

Investment Bonds

Investment Bonds are single premium life insurance contract that buy investments on the investors behalf, in a similar way to Unit Trusts. While the principal is similar to Unit Trusts, an Investment Bond differs greatly in the way that it is taxed. Where a Unit Trust is taxed under Capital Gains Tax rules, an Investment Bond is taxed under Income Tax rules. This can have advantages and disadvantages depending on your circumstances, and it is in this area that you must ensure that you take professional advice.

There are many other forms of collective investment, but they are simply versions of the above schemes. You can, for example, invest in an Investment Bond off-shore. This means that you will receive gross roll-up on the gains, and will only be taxed when you bring the investments into the UK. However, all other schemes are simply versions of the above. They may mix in different types of investment, such as options, to produce guaranteed bonds, or investments, but principally, these are the basic 5 types of collective investment.

Choosing an investment

Your choice of investment will depend greatly on your own personal circumstances. In particular your view towards investment risk, the amount that you are investing and your present and future taxation circumstances.

As a general rule, you should invest in collective investments if you are investing under £50,000. If you are investing over £50,000 then you can look at direct equity investments if you have the time. Investments into property should only be taken on if you have the time to deal with the work involved and if you are looking to accelerate your financial plan. (See the chapter on accelerating you financial plan.)

My suggestion in making investments is that you seek advice. A quality Independent Financial Adviser (IFA) will be able to help in this area.

In my experience, people often try to make investment decisions themselves, based on the advice given in the financial sections of the newspapers. People, will invest simply by looking at the advertisements in the newspapers placed by investments companies! In fact, I've known people even believe what is written in the newspapers!

The two points to understand here is that firstly you are not looking at a newspaper, but an opinion paper. You are reading simply what the financial journalist's opinions are. Under the terms of the Financial Services Act, newspapers are excluded from liability on the 'advice' that they give. This means that you have no comeback if you take their advice and it is wrong. Take for example the so-called 'mis-selling' of pensions in the eighties. If an IFA had advised you to buy a pension and the advice was wrong then you had recourse against that IFA, and would receive compensation from them. If, however, you had taken the newspapers advice, and it was wrong, then you would have no comeback. Clearly it is better to have protection than not.

Secondly, have you ever noticed that every investments, company seems to advertise itself as the best? They all seem to have awards to demonstrate their ability and can show how their particular fund is better than any other. Well, as the saying goes, "there are lies, damn lies and statistics". In fact, you can make just about any reasonable investment fund look good by changing the basis of the valuation. By simply changing the measurement dates by a few days can make a massive amount of difference to the funds measured performance. This is a trick often used in newspaper adverts. Take a look at the adverts and in the small print you will see how some of the strangest date comparisons are used.

A good quality IFA will see through this. A good IFA will have computer systems that wash away this biased information and will allow accurate, fund on fund comparisons.

And yes it is true, you will have to pay for this advice. This will either be in the form of a fee to the IFA or a payment of commission to the IFA from the investment provider, either way the IFA must be paid. However, what you will find is that, providing the IFA is good, they will be able to negotiate better terms for you than if you dealt with the company direct. This will usually mean that you will save money, even if the IFA is receiving a commission.

The important thing to remember is that you get good long-term performance, that matches your view towards risk and reward, and that provides the best tax advantages to you. These are complicated issues and unless you are dealing with them on a full time basis then you must seek help. Paying an IFA is an investment in your financial future not a cost. Every single millionaire that you meet will have a good adviser. That is because they know the value of the advice. They also understand that "if you pay peanuts, then you will get monkeys"!

Chapter 11   More Investing

You now have a good understanding of investments, and if you have fully understood and worked through the previous chapter you probably have as good an idea as the majority of people regarding investments. However, life is not as simple as that. Yes you can achieve some great returns on your investments using the ideas in the previous chapter, but if you want to be a serious investor you need to understand more about the strategies involved in developing an investment portfolio.

Developing an investment portfolio is only something you can do once you have some money to put into a portfolio. It goes without saying that you must have some money before you start to invest. So how much do you need before you can start working on your own investment portfolio? The answer is probably about six months worth of income. Broadly speaking this will be the amount that can be held in the income account. Remember you need to build your Capital account first before you work on your Income account. Once this is done you

103

can then develop your assets to produce financial independence. Remember investing means using asset backed investments rather than deposit based investments. Asset backed investments are those investments that have the ability to out-pace inflation and give you real returns on your investments. But you should only do this if you have sufficient funds on deposit in your capital account first.

Lets assume then, that you have built up your Capital account, and are now ready to invest for your Income account and then ultimately your funds for financial independence. Where do you start?

The vast majority of people know how to invest, and how to develop an investment strategy. Unfortunately, the problem is that virtually no one does what they know they should do. Successful investing is the result of commonsense mixed with the understanding of very sound financial principles and an understanding of the taxation system.

You see, investing is just like dieting. Everyone really does know what to do to lose weight. It is simply a process of eating less of the wrong food but more of the right food. This means carefully controlling what and when you eat and when and how you exercise. However, people don't do what they know. They are always looking for the next greatest diet, or the best diet club, or the newest diet system with its special shakes and soups. People do all these things but forget the basics of "eat less and exercise more". This is exactly how people are when they are looking to invest. People spend their time looking for the latest and greatest investment, they spend their time looking for the best investment tip, and they get involved in speculation.

The secrets of developing an effective investment strategy are very simple. They involve using an existing strategy that is proven and works. It involves buying low and selling high, it involves avoiding as much tax as is possible and it involves taking advice where you need it.

In the book 'The Millionaire Next Door' by Dr Thomas J. Stanley and William D. Danko (Longstreet Press, 1996) the authors interviewed 773 individual millionaires. The objective was to ascertain what these people had in common. What the research showed is that millionaires do not check the markets every day, they don't trade or buy and sell often. They each have a systematic approach to investing. These approaches could even be described as boring, but, in the world of investing, boring is good.

In this chapter we are going to look at each area of investing. By the time you have finished here you will understand more than the average stockbroker and investment adviser. The knowledge that I pass to you can be used either by yourself, or with your Financial Adviser to develop you financial portfolio.

As with previous chapters it is important to work through this chapter in order as each section builds on the previous section. It is like baking a cake, you don't just need all the ingredients, you need to know the order that they go into the mix and in what quantities, without reading in order you may find that you get a spongy mess rather than a nice Victoria sponge!

In this chapter, I will concentrate on developing an investment strategy that works. While the rest of this book shows you the strategies involved in becoming seriously wealthy, this chapter tells you what to do when you've got it, what to do to keep it and how to build it. Now, while developing a strategy is relatively simple, it is not necessarily easy. It takes dedication, it takes a little bit of time, being honest with yourself, and knowing when to get help. So lets start here. When should you get help and where do you get it from?

Asking for Help

There has been a great deal of poor information in the media of late. Most of this is not the journalists fault, indeed a good financial journalist will understand the points that I am making and will be aware of the report to which I will refer. Unfortunately, a large portion of the media have not done their research before going to print. Other journalists then take what the first journalist said as gospel and simply regurgitate it. I am sure you will recall the headlines in the press and the articles in the Sunday papers saying how, "actively managed investments did not perform well against peoples own self-invested investments". You will also remember the statements that, "investment charges eat into your investments and cause your investments to perform poorly". However, this is not the case. You can see in the following chart overleaf, the results of some interesting research. The Dalbar Study looked at investments made between 1/1/84 and 31/12/95. The study looked at the effects of advice and the effects of investments with 'up front' charges. The results speak for themselves. While the returns of 'No Load' funds without an adviser produced a return of 98%, 'loaded' funds with an adviser produced a return of

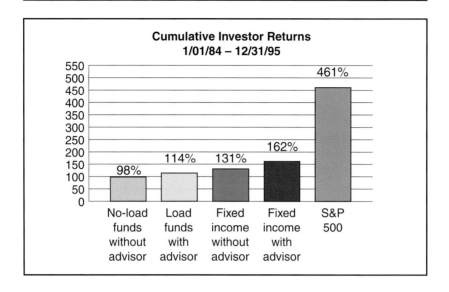

114%. Fixed income investments without an adviser produced a return over the period of 131%, and those with an adviser produced a return of 162%. This means that funds with an up front charge produce a return 16% greater over the period. Those investments with an adviser produced a return of over 23% higher.

Does this mean that you should only invest in an investment with an upfront charge and that you should only invest in an investment that is recommended by an advisor? Of course not. But what it does do is to demonstrate that you need to consider all the alternatives before investing and not to be knocked off track by the comments of the media, especially when you consider that the media is exempt from financial services regulation and carries no investor protection, which is given by advisors.

So when you are developing your investment strategy, and when you are looking to make investments consider in what areas you need help. Do you need help simply to review your existing investments so that the new investments can be structured to complement or balance the existing investments? Do you need help to consider the relative taxation consequences of your actions? Or do you need help with the entire process of investing, and want to leave the process to a professional you can trust and rely on? Which ever area it is, be honest enough with yourself and ask an adviser and or course make sure it is the right adviser.

The Four Foundations of Investing

There are four things to consider when developing an investment strategy:

1. Purpose

2. Time Horizon

3. Risk Levels and Portfolio Construction.

4. Asset Allocation

Purpose and Time Horizon

Most people tend to invest because they have the money to invest. Very rarely do they know why they are investing. This is probably the number one reason why people are unsuccessful in investing, not because they don't have the right strategy and not because they don't know how, but because they don't know why they are investing.

Unless you know how long you intend to invest for, it is impossible to develop a successful investment strategy. If you are going to invest for two years you will develop a different strategy to that which you are going to invest in for ten years. The term of an investment will have a substantial impact on your portfolio as the term will not only dictate the investments that you are going to use, but also the effect of taxation payable.

Risk Levels

The levels of risk that you are prepared to accept will also have a massive impact on your investment portfolio. Clearly someone with a low tolerance to investment risk will invest in a totally different way to someone who has a high tolerance to investment risk. Unlike with the chapter on savings, risk with regard to lump sum investing should be thought of in a different way.

Asset Allocation

Research has shown that asset allocation has the greatest impact on an investments performance. It is more important than stock selection, investment vehicle selection and charges. Asset allocation is the process whereby your portfolio is divided into separate areas to avoid

'Having all your eggs in one basket'. This process is so important they even award prizes to people who get it right.

Portfolio Construction

Once you have taken the three areas of purpose, term and risk into account you actually need to construct your portfolio. Constructing a portfolio is a simple process once you have decided upon the strategy that you will use. The important thing here is to select the right investment strategy.

Let's now move on to consider Each of these areas and start to develop an investment strategy that matches what you need not only to make your assets grow, but also to protect them from falling markets.

Purpose

As I said earlier, it is virtually impossible to develop an investment portfolio unless you have first decided what you want it to achieve, and what your goals are then we can develop the correct strategy for you.

At this stage you should go back to the chapters on 'The Why'. If you have fully completed the exercises then it will be relatively easy to decide on your objectives. If you have not, then go back now and complete them, it will make the rest of this chapter much easier to use.

When deciding on the purpose of the investment it will usually fall into one of four areas:

1. Investing for income

2. Investing for a specific purpose

3. Investing to pass on a legacy

4. Investing for Financial Security

1. Investing for Income

If you are investing for income then you are usually investing to provide that income immediately. If this is the case you need to consider two separate points. Firstly how much income do you need? This will affect the 'Hurdle Rate' that you need the investments to produce.

For example, if you need an income of £5000 and you have £100,000 to invest, then you will need a return – a Hurdle Rate – of 5%. However, this is not the case if you need the income to increase each year, to keep pace with inflation, for example. If this is what you need then you need a higher Hurdle Rate because you need the funds to grow in addition to the income required. The additional income will then be set aside to increase the capital so that it, in turn can produce a higher future yield. In this example you will then need a Hurdle Rate of around 6.5%. The £100,000 would then produce a return of £6500 pa. From this you will take £5000 and set aside £1500 for future capital growth, that will produce additional yield.

The second thing to consider when deciding upon your goals in relation to investing for income is the taxation situation.

The effects of taxation have the most dramatic effect on you investments. Taxation affects your investments much more then the return of the investments and charges that are associated with them. IF you are paying the top rate of tax, then this will have a massive effect when compared to paying no tax. For this reason, you must construct your portfolio in the most tax efficient way possible. This is one of the areas where you must seek professional advice. Tax rules change to quickly for me to offer specific advice in this area and so, unless you are extremely knowledgeable and competent, get some help. However, even the best advisers and accountants sometimes forget basic tax planning strategy in relation to developing investments. Basic tax planning strategy for investments that are designed to produce an income, is that you take income in the following order:

- From assets that produce tax free income

- From assets that produce a return that can be set against capital gains rather than income

- From assets that are tax advantageous

- From assets that are tax deferred

- From assets that are taxed

2. Investing for a Specific Purpose

Investing for a specific purpose is probably the easiest purpose to develop an investment for. This is because you will usually know the time that the investment proceeds will be needed and you will also know the amount that is needed. As you know these two facts, it is relatively easy to work out, the amount that you must invest and/or the rate of return (Hurdle Rate) that must be achieved.

For example, if you need £10,000 to pay for your daughters' wedding in ten years time, and you have £5000 to be invested, you can calculate that you need to achieve a Hurdle Rate of 7.2%. If however, you feel that 7.2% was unachievable based on the levels of risk that you want to take, then you can calculate that at a Hurdle Rate of 5%, you need to invest £6200.

The important point here is to ensure that you have as accurate an idea as possible of the dates when the money is needed and the amount that will be needed.

3. Investing to Pass On a Legacy

Some people are quite happy with their levels of income and the security that the investments they hold will meet their future requirements and so will often invest to pass a legacy to children, grandchildren or a charity. In this case there are two important considerations. The first is that of life expectancy as the legacy will be passed in the event of death, then the portfolio must be constructed based on your assumed life expectancy.

Age Now	55	60	65	70
Men	28	23	17	15
Women	31	26	21	19
Joint	36	28	25	23
Souce: CMIB of Institute of Actuaries 3/1/02				

The following chart shows the life expectancy of both men, women and a couple.

You can see from this chart that a man aged 55 has a life expectancy of another 28 years, taking him to age 83. A man aged 70 has a life expectancy of 85. The point to note here is that as a person gets older, their life expectancy gets longer. You can also see that a couple living together have a longer life expectancy still. This is based on the second death.

I recall one client who wanted to leave a sum to their grandchildren. The grandchildren were in their early teens, the clients were in their early seventies. The clients wanted the grandchildren to have a sum of money on their death. As the clients were in their early seventies they believed that they had a life expectancy of three to four years. Both clients were fit and healthy and had no reason to believe that they might fall ill in the near future. When we look-up their life expectancy it suggest that they are, actuarially, likely to live for a further 18 years or so. That being the case three questions were raised. Did they want to wait a further 18 odd years before passing the funds to their grandchildren? If they were going to wait 18 years or so, then their investment strategy would be based on an 18 year term not the original 3 to 5 year term. Also, if they were statistically likely to live for another 18 years, they could either invest less than originally planned or pass on more than originally planned?

4. Investing for Financial Security

From my experience, over 70% of people are actually investing for financial security. The majority do not actually need the money now, and are unlikely to need it in the future, but like the warm, cosy feeling they get inside knowing that they have enough money to do what they want, when they want. That being the case then they are, in fact, investing for their lifetime and so need to construct an investment portfolio based upon their life expectancy.

Risk Levels

Risk levels are often confused with volatility. Risk and volatility are very closely related, but they are different.

Risk denotes that long term danger, that capital and growth may be lost. Volatility denotes the day-to-day, week-to-week, and month-to-month movement in the capital.

Let's take an example. If you were to buy shares in a very strong Blue Chip FTSE100 company that has a great trading history, has a good free asset ratio, it would not be that risky. This is because, generally, the value of the shares would grow based upon the growth and profitability of the company, thus allowing the value of the stock to keep pace with inflation. However, the stock would probably be very volatile. That means that on a day-to-day, week-to-week and month-to-month basis, the value of the stock would fluctuate. Now, this is not to say that there is no risk in holding the shares in the company, of course there is, but understanding the general difference between risk and volatility will help you later on when I go on to explain The Advanced Investment Strategy©.

The levels of risk that you take will be a function of your attitudes and your requirements. It will be your attitude that ultimately decides the level of risk that you will take, but it is your requirements that dictate how much risk you must take.

For example, consider the earlier situation where £5,000 of income was required, and the client had £100,000 to invest leaving a basic Hurdle Rate of 5%. To produce a return over a long period of time is relatively easy to do, and so not a great deal of risk need to be taken. However, imagine that the situation was different. Imagine that you needed to produce the £5,000 return, but only had £70,000 to invest. Assuming that you did not want to erode your capital you would then need to produce a Hurdle Rate of 7.1%. If you only had £50,000 to invest then you would need to produce a Hurdle Rate of 10%. This will mean taking a much greater risk than earlier.

The point to note is that everyone gets it wrong, everyone seems to say, "he can take a risk he can afford to lose it". This is wrong, you see if he has enough money then he does not need to take any risk at all. It is only those people that do not have the money that must take a risk, as it is the only way that they will achieve their goals

Asset Allocation

Asset Allocation is spreading your assets around to avoid having all your eggs in one basket. However, the process of doing this can be extremely complicated. The important thing here is to make sure that you understand the general process and then find assets that fall into the categories that you require, based upon The Advanced Investment Strategy©.

I have searched for many years to find an Asset Allocation strategy that meets both my requirements and that of my clients. The best system that I have found is based upon the work of Harry Markowitz. Harry Markowitz received the Nobel Prize for economics in 1990 for developing an investment strategy. Now there are not many people that have won a Nobel Prize and so I think it only fair that we consider how the Markowitz Model works and how we can use it to improve our own investment performance.

The Markowitz Model is based on the theory of 'correlation diversification'. Correlation is the degree to which an asset has a relationship with another asset. Diversification is the process of ensuring the correlation is low.

Here is an example. Imagine two products, sun tan lotion and umbrellas. As a general rule people only buy sun tan lotion when it is sunny. There is no need for the product when the weather is dull and overcast. Conversely, people only buy umbrellas when they expect it to rain. The purchasing patterns for umbrellas and sun tan lotion are then diametrically opposed. This means that when there is a great demand for sun tan lotion, there is probably a low demand for umbrellas and visa versa.

Take another example, that of hamburgers. If the demand for fast food were to increase across the globe both MacDonald's and Burger King would benefit. This is because they have a high correlation. In effect, the increased sale of hamburgers in MacDonald's is often mirrored by increased sales in Burger King.

This means that there is a low correlation between sun tan lotion sales and umbrella sales and a high correlation between MacDonald's and Burger King. If you therefore wanted to spread the risk of your investment portfolio you would avoid buying into investments that had a high correlation, and would look to buy investments that had a low correlation.

Markowitz pointed out that there are basically four different asset classes. These asset classes are Cash, Bonds, Equities and Property.

Cash is all assets that are deposit based. This means that there is no risk to the capital, and that the only real risks are the capital being lost if the institution holding the funds goes out of business, or the real value of the money being eroded by inflation.

Bonds are assets that are invested in Government gilts and corporate bonds. A bond is really a loan. It is a loan to an institution, be it the government or a company. The company or the government agree to pay a specified level of interest for a specified period and at the maturity date, pay back the capital. These investments are relatively low risk, although the level of risk depends on the issuing institution.

Equities are stocks and shares in listed and unlisted companies. With equities you effectively own a 'share' in the company. As such you are entitled to a 'share' of the profits, known as dividends. Equities provide the highest level of risk of all the investment classes.

Property is the final asset class. This can be both commercial or private.

Asset allocation is all about deciding how much you want to invest in each area. It is this asset allocation process that has a dramatic impact on your growth prospects.

A further point to consider is a regular change in the make up of your portfolio to keep your asset allocation correctly balanced. I will cover this more in the section on Portfolio Construction. However the general principal is to 'lock in your gains' when you have made them. For example, if you have an investment that has produced a return of, say 25% in one year, you should consider taking the gain on that investment and moving to a new lower risk investment. Now, this will mean that you may lose out on further growth in the investment, which is why you do not sell it all, but by moving the gain into a lower risk investment, you lock in the gains and massively reduce the possible loss that can be made if the value of the investment falls.

Portfolio Construction

We have now thought about our purpose, we know how long we are likely to invest for and we have an idea of the levels of risk that we want to take. The next stage is to actually start developing our portfolio.

I believe that the best way to construct a portfolio is to start with the perfect design for you, and then overlay the existing portfolio and investments that you have onto it. You can then see what areas must be changed and which areas work.

I find that, as a general rule, clients take too much risk with their money. They feel that they must take a risk to make a decent return. Alternatively, a great many clients think they are not taking a big risk but are, simply because they do not fully understand the investments they have, or do not understand the level of risk associated with their investments.

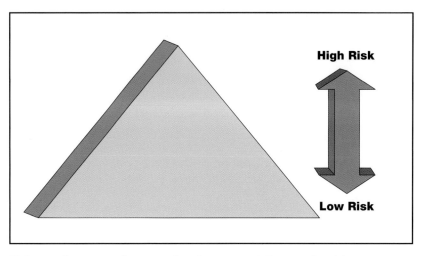

If this is the case, when we develop a portfolio we should structure it like a triangle.

For most people it is sensible to restrict risk, this means investing more in lower risk investment than in higher risk investments. You can see from the above diagram a typical investor. This investor has a choice of either depositing money and taking no capital risk at all, this is the bottom line of the triangle, or taking a risk and investing anywhere within the triangle.

The higher the person gets in the triangle, the more risk he will take. It is for this reason that he should invest less as he moves up the triangle. The idea of the triangle is that it easily shows the relationship between

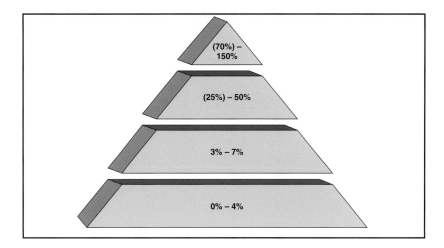

the amount that should be invested and the level of risk that you should take together with the potential annual growth (or loss) that can be achieved.

In this next diagram, I have overlaid the type of investment that generally meet the levels of risk on the triangle. You can see from this that the most secure way of holding money is in Governments Deposits. These deposits are backed by the Government and are safer than any bank. The highest risk investment is the use of warrants or options. With warrants or options you can either gain a great deal or you can lose a great deal.

Obviously the world of investing is more involved than this, but this is

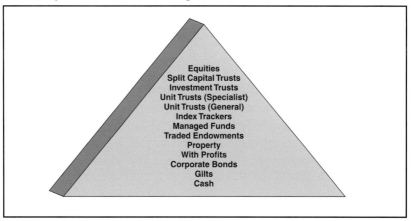

Equities
Split Capital Trusts
Investment Trusts
Unit Trusts (Specialist)
Unit Trusts (General)
Index Trackers
Managed Funds
Traded Endowments
Property
With Profits
Corporate Bonds
Gilts
Cash

a good start. It does not mean that you should invest in every area available. What it does is to give you a graphical understanding of what should be considered in developing an investment portfolio, along with an idea of what to ask for when you speak to an adviser.

If you have considered your purpose in detail, you will know the Hurdle Rate that you need or want to achieve. This rate overlaid onto the above diagram, will then give you a strong feeling for the types of investment that you should consider.

The next stage is for you to consider what risk you really are going to take. Probably the best way to do this is to simplify the diagram down into four.

The first part, the section at the bottom, is for 'No risk' investments. In fact these are not investments but are funds on deposit. The second area is for low risk investments. These are investments where there is very little risk to capital. This will include some bonds, depending on the issuing institution and some property. The medium risk area has a larger risk to capital. This will include higher risk bonds, some high risk property investments and lower risk equities, such as large blue chip companies. The final high risk area has a very large risk to the capital. This will include the majority of equity investments.

You must now decide how much of your money you are going to keep on deposit. As you can only reasonably expect a return of 3%-4% in this area prior to tax, you should keep the minimum that is required to meet you cash emergency needs. Of course if you only need a Hurdle Rate of 3% you can keep your money on deposit. On the assumption that you will require a much greater return than this you will have to make investments in the other areas.

For a 'typical' client the remainder of their funds would be split with 50% in low risk, 30% in medium risk and 20% in high risk. Now, this may not be the case for you but it is a good starting point. The important thing here is to split your money up into the areas of risk that you want. Once you have made this decision, it is vital that you continue to review the portfolio to ensure that as assets grow you continue to 'rebase' your investments. This is the process I spoke of earlier where you 'lock in the gain' you have made by amending investment mixes to bring them back to the way you want them balanced.

The final stage is the process of actually choosing the investment that you are going to buy. This process that I strongly recommend is The Advanced Investment Strategy©.

The Advanced Investment Strategy©

The Advanced Investment Strategy was developed over a two year period at Wills and Trusts Independent Financial Planning, my financial planning company. We were aware of most of the investment selection processes but had never been comfortable with any of them. Many were good with regards to selecting individual shares and equities, such as Jim Slaters 'Zulu' system. Others were good for selection of unit trusts and investment bonds. However I have never found a system that was simple enough to explain to all my clients and successful enough to produce the results that I wanted. The solution, therefore was to design an investment strategy from scratch, which is what we have done with The Advanced Investment Strategy. This system is used by all our clients and many other planners in the financial services business I have trained, but this is the first time that it has been published.

It was designed to cater for all types of investments. This means that you can use it in the selection process for stocks and shares, for property, for bonds, in fact for any investment vehicle. It was also designed so that anyone can use it. Obviously it will be easier for a practising financial adviser to use as the adviser will have all the required information to hand, however, anyone, who has access to a computer, can find the relevant information and construct their own investment portfolio.

It was also designed to be effective over the long term and the short term. Most investment strategies focus on the long term, which is fine, but there are times when a strategy that can be used for the short term is needed.

Component Parts of The Advanced Investment Strategy©

The Advanced Investment Strategy is broken down into two separate areas:

1. Performance

2. Volatility

Each of these areas is a filter in the selection process and should be used in the above order. This means that you first use the performance filter on the investment that you are considering. If the investment passes this hurdle you then place it against the volatility filter. It is vital to remember that the chosen investment must pass each of the filters. It is not a case of passing one out of two, just because you like the investment. It must pass both. Now, the only areas where you may not use The Advanced Investment Strategy is in the selection of individual shares. In this case you can use the stock selection process outlined in the earlier chapter. You will find that the results will be the same. However it is good to use the stock selection process mentioned previously because it will give you a better understanding of the company in which you intend to purchase shares. The Advanced Investment Strategy absolutely must be uses, when purchasing collective investments such as unit trusts, investment bonds and investments trusts etc.

Performance

You will all know that "past performance is not necessarily a guide to the future" as the UK financial services regulator reminds us. The point to note here is the word necessarily since there is always a relationship between past performance and future performance, the trick is finding that relationship. If there were not a relationship then the bookmakers of the world would be out of business.

Take English football, for example. If you had to bet on which football team were to win the FA cup at the beginning of the year, and you had two choices, Manchester United and Aylesbury United (Aylesbury United is a small part time team that comes from the town where I live) you would probably bet on Manchester United to win. Now, they will not necessarily win, but the chances of them winning are much better than Aylesbury United. After all, Manchester United have won before, therefore they have experience to fall back on. They have expensive players, who have the ability to play extraordinarily well. Now all of these things do not mean that they will win, or that Aylesbury United will not win, but there is a very strong pointer as to who may win.

The same is true of investments, take buying shares in a company for example. If you had the choice of buying shares in one of the worlds largest and strongest banks or to buy shares in a brand new company which had no trading history and was going into uncharted waters as far as markets were concerned, who would you put the majority of your money on?

So you can see that past performance is some measure of potential future success, but the difficult point is measuring this correctly and using it in the right way.

The Advanced Investment Strategy, states that you can only invest in those investments that have produced a return above the sector average when measured over 1, 3 and 5 years.

This means that you must find the investment and sector performer that compares favourably over the measured period and you only invest in that investment which produces a return above the sector average on the one, three and five year points. If at any time during those periods it falls below the average, then you disregard it.

Why do we measure it over one, three and five years? The answer is three fold. Firstly, the economies of the world have substantially changed over the least decade. For this reason the statistics of ten years ago are not as relevant as they once were. The second point is that, while it is relatively easy to provide performance that is good over one year, it is very tough to produce that performance on a consistent basis. It is for this reason that one, three and five years must be reviewed. Finally, if an investment performs, above average, it must be better than the average.

When comparing performance it is vital that you use independent figures to measure the performance. You may have noticed that the majority of investments that advertise in the press are always terrific performers. Very rarely do you see an advertisement saying that you should buy this investment because it was the worst in its class. Unfortunately, it is relatively easy to manipulate the performance figures on investments by changing the time period over which the investment is measured. Because of the volatility of investments you can increase or decrease the apparent investment performance by changing the valuation point by a few days. It is for this reason that you must get totally independent performance figures. These figures should all be measured on the same basis. This means that the measurement point should be the same in each case. My personal favourite is 1st January to 31st December each year. I find this easy to think about and easy to measure.

The effect of applying this filter is that you very quickly and efficiently get rid of the poor performers and are left with the good consistent performers. When you apply this filter you will find that, you will be left with between 20% and 30% of the investments that you are reviewing.

Once you have completed this filter you can move onto the next, 'Volatility'.

Volatility

We use volatility as a filter because it can be used to rid us of those investments too risky to hold. The volatility figure for most investments is widely published and can be found in most of the trade press and individual providers web sites.

Volatility is the degree to which an investments value moves both positively and negatively. The volatility figure is based on a mathematical variance called 'standard deviation'. Now, unless you want to be a very highly qualified investment adviser you do not really need to know how this figure is calculated. All you really need to understand is that the volatility figure is the degree to which an investment will vary from the average. So if the average return on an investment is 8% and there is a volatility rating of 3% the actual investment has performed between 5% and 11% over the three year period, giving an average of 8%.

To put this into perspective, imagine the above investment and imagine another investment with an average return of 8% but with a volatility rating of 4%. Which would you choose. The answer is clearly the first. This is because the second investment, while producing the same average return, can have the actual yearly figure swing between 4% and 12%. Clearly, with single investments we want stability and we do not want the value of the investment to swing from one extreme to the other.

With volatility we only use those investment that are:

Below average volatility

This means that we must look at the volatility figures and then compare them to the average for the same period. Any investment that has a higher level of volatility than the average is discarded. The effect of this filter means that you will immediately get rid of the higher risk investments, those where your capital is at serious risk. This does mean that you will discard the best performers, but that is because the best performers are also the most risky performers.

Applying this filter to investments is that you will be left with another 20% to 30% of the investments. The effect of applying the two filters to your investments is truly staggering.

In the UK we have access to around 17,500 different investments. If you apply the two filters to these 17,500 investments you will be left with around 50. Yes, you read that correctly, 50 investments only out of 17,500 meet the requirements of The Advanced Investment Strategy!

You will see from this the power of The Advanced Investment Strategy. It appears on the face of it to be surprisingly simple, but the reality is that it is incredibly powerful at weeding out the poor and average performers, and attracting the consistent, high performers.

Summary

You have now identified what it is you want to achieve and the levels of risk that you are prepared to take. You have decided what sort of investments you want to invest in and the classes of investments you want to use. You have also used The Advanced Investment Strategy to select from those asset classes the investments that are to be used.

You are now in the position to put your plan in place and purchase those investments that you have fully investigated and reviewed in the knowledge that you will be developing an effective and successful strategy.

Chapter 12   Accelerating Your Plan

Doug

Over the years you will build your capital mass and thus your Financial Independence through saving and investing part of your income. Over the years this will provide total Financial Independence and make you seriously wealthy if you use the ideas and techniques explained in previous chapters. However, it is possible to accelerate your plan and reach Financial Independence in a much shorter time scale.

Doing this can be risky but if used correctly you can accelerate your plan and bring Financial Independence in a few short years, but a few words of warning? If you have a risk rating of 6 or less then this is not for you. It is imperative to understand that what follows is a high risk strategy of reaching Financial Independence very quickly. High risk means that things can go wrong, and I have seen them go wrong, so do not be carried away with the idea of great riches quickly. You must have a level head and a steady nerve to use these techniques.

Before you accelerate your plan

The first point to consider is where you are in developing your financial plan? I firmly believe that you must first set up the necessary areas of financial protection before you embark on this area of your financial plan. I also believe that you must have both a Capital Account and Income Account in place before you commit any funds to this high-risk area. Now, I know of a number of people who have been very successful at developing Financial Independence who have not had either a Capital Account or Income Account in place when they set to work on these areas, but I have also seen a number of people lose everything. For this reason **please** do not start on this area until the basics are in place.

How do you accelerate your Financial Plan?

There is one primary technique that can be used in a number of ways to accelerate you plan and this is the technique known as GEARING.

Gearing is a term that accountants use to describe procedures that increase the results of a transaction. In terms of what we are trying to achieve this means using either 'Other Peoples Money' (OPM) or using 'Derivatives', often called 'Futures and Options'.

The principal is similar for each of the two techniques, but each is suited to different people depending on their cultural and educational background.

Using OPM

In the past many people have advocated borrowing to invest. Unfortunately, this has developed a bad name as people have borrowed to "buy the latest hot stock" but found that the stock was not what it had appeared to be, resulting in them losing money, and on top of that, having interest to pay.

I do not advocate borrowing money to invest in stock no matter how good a deal it may seem to be. Unless you are a full time trader, you will be the last person to hear of any great deal going about. In the financial world, there will be thousands of other people who would have had the information before you and have acted upon it. It is virtually impossible to make a 'fast buck' this way and borrowing to do it will only increase the problem.

In my opinion there is only one investment transaction that you should consider borrowing money for, and that is to buy property.

Investing in property, when using OPM, can dramatically increase your critical mass, provided it is done in a calculated manner. You must understand that this technique is time consuming, and will take some practice. As such you should perhaps aim for a small gain initially and work up to better results. Part of the problem with this type of system is that people can become greedy very easily, and this is often when things go wrong.

First it is important to understand the principles involved and then we can look at the practicalities. Let's do this by looking at an example.

Assume for a moment that you have £10,000 to invest and that you are happy that you have a Capital and Income Account and are keen to use a higher risk investment to accelerate your plan.

You have identified the right property and have agreed to purchase the property for £50,000, using your £10,000 and by borrowing £40,000 to finance the rest of the purchase. Once you have purchased the property you have to make repayments to the mortgage company of £300 per month, and so you lease the property out for £350 per month to cover the mortgage repayment and the additional costs involved in arranging the rental. At the end of the year you sell the property for £55,000, after costs, as the property has increased in value by 10%. However, your gain is not 10%, it is 50%, i.e., a return of £15,000 on an initial investment of £10,000, making a gain of 50% in one year.

This example demonstrates in a simple form how gearing or borrowing to accelerate your return can generate fantastic growth results. When I explain this simple example to people they often think that this is a low risk adventure as the assets are covered by real property. But this misses the point. You see, if there was a fall in the property market and the value of the property fell to £45,000 then, while there has only been a 5% fall in property prices, the investor will have made a 50% loss.

There are also two important considerations. Firstly, with a property investment you are tying up your funds for a fixed period and it can be very hard to release these funds in an emergency. Secondly, these type of arrangements do take up a large amount of time and effort, but if you are happy to accept these disadvantages, then they can have a dramatic impact on your financial plan.

How to put property purchase and OPM into action

Now that you understand the principals involved you can work through the steps involved. However, the process of buying property to generate capital gain is worthy of a book in itself, in fact there are a number of excellent books which cover this area in detail. If you are going to take part in this type of activity I strongly suggest that you do some further independent research, to gain other peoples' thoughts and ideas.

Step one – Establish the geographical area in which you want to buy

This is a very important point. As property agents say, there are three things to consider when you purchase a property, 'location, location, location'. I recommend using an area that you can travel to easily and quickly, ideally within fifteen minutes of home. This will allow you to keep an eye on any tenants that you may rent to, also you will probably have a better idea of the movement in property prices in you own area as opposed to other areas.

Step two – Establish if you want a capital gain or income

There are two ways that you can deal with property. Either you can buy it to make a capital gain and then sell it, or you can buy it to rent out and generate an income.

I know of a number of advisers who advocate the second option for building financial independence. This involves buying a number of properties and then renting each out in such a way that the rental generated is in excess of the mortgage payment made, the difference being your increased net income.

It would work in this way. Say, you had £5000 to invest. You would use this to buy a property for £50,000, borrowing £45,000. The property would then be rented out to generate an income. If the income on the rental was £400 per month and the mortgage payment £250 per month, then you would have £150 per month to re-invest in another property. You would continue to add additional properties until the income that you received in rental payments, over and above the mortgage costs would be net income. Carrying the example forward, if you need net income each month of £1500 to meet your requirements, then you would need 10 similar properties to rent out to generate this income. This would require about £50,000 in initial capital. Obviously, in the real world it does not always work out his way as you have costs, taxation and administration to contend with, but the principle is sound.

I do not, however, advocate this system. I feel that it ties up capital to a greater degree than is sensible. Also there is a massive time investment in both administering the rentals as well as looking after the properties. While this system may work well in the USA it does not seem to work that well in the UK. This is principally because there is a culture of renting in the USA but not so in the UK, where there is a general belief that it is best to buy. This means that it is the poorer and lower financially stable people that rent in the UK and you are much more likely to have rent collection problems than is the case in the USA.

I believe it is best to purchase a property with the purpose of selling it, once a reasonable profit has been made. As we have a capital gains allowance in the UK, (this being the amount of profit on a capital transaction that you can make before you pay tax. In this case £7100 in the 99/00 tax year) I suggest that this should be your gain target. So if you buy a property for £50,000, you can sell it for £57100, after all costs, you should then sell it and bank the gain and place the profit either in a new property or in a more liquid investment. It is fine to rent out a property while you are waiting for it to appreciate, but buy the property to sell.

Step three – Choose good agents

As time goes by you will be buying, selling and renting out a number of properties and so will be generating a great deal of business for the estate and leasing agents. It therefore makes sense to find a decent agent to handle all your business. If they know that you will be placing all of your business with them then arrange an advantageous deal to reduce their commissions and charges or the basis that they will be your sole agents.

Step four – Decide on the capital available

You must decide how much capital you want to use in this area of your financial plan. It is important to bear in mind that this will be the least liquid part of your financial plan, so I urge you to be conservative. Please ensure that you have a sufficient capital account at the very least before embarking on a property purchase. I have never seen a property purchase that did not cost more than the original budget, and you would be no different, so add a contingency fund or float to you calculations when working out your budgets.

Step five – Find the right property

Finding the right property is extremely important. The most important thing to remember with this is that you are buying the property as a business proposition, not as a place of residence. This means that you must consider three factors buying the property.

1. The resaleability of the property. It is no good buying a property that is a 'super deal' if it will be difficult to resell. If it is that good a deal, then you must ask yourself why? Have the vendors had trouble selling it for some reason, is there a problem with the structure of the house, are there neighbors from hell next door?

2. The rentability. How easy is it going to be to rent out? Is it in an area with good parking, near to the town centre or within the local school's catchment area?

3. Work required. Work is required on the property to make it suitable for rental. As a landlord you will be responsible for all repairs, be they minor or major. Do you want to have the tenants calling you at 8:00pm on a Sunday evening because there is a problem with the heating system.

Step six – Buy and rent

Obtaining a mortgage on this type of property can be difficult, and so I recommend that you use your independent financial adviser. Please understand, there are a number of mortgage brokers who will profess to be independent but are linked to a life insurance company, so limiting the options for arranging the relevant life insurance to cover the loan. It is, therefore, a good idea to use an IFA that will work for you and not for the companies involved. You should expect to pay a fee for this, that way you will not be limited in any way to the mortgage companies that are being used. £250 – £400 is about the right cost, depending where you live. Also budget for solicitors fees of about £300 and rental fees to about 10% of the rental fee.

In buying the property it is important to remember that you are buying it to make a profit. This means that you need to negotiate the best possible price. This is not a popularity race, the object is to buy the property for the lowest possible price. Do not be afraid of offering what may be considered a low price, you can always increase your offer, but you can not realistically reduce it (unless, for example the survey points out problems in the property – when you should work hard to get the price reduced) Do not 'fall in love' with the property. It is easy to find what you think is the best possible property, but it may be over priced. You will be so keen to get underway with your plan that you may buy at an unrealistic price. I have made this mistake myself. I was keen to make my first property purchase and agreed what I considered to be a good price of £65,000. However, the valuation came in at £55,000. I attempted to renogotiate the price but the vendor would not budge. I, therefore, agreed to pay the full price of £65,000, thinking that I could make this up when I sold the property. Unfortunately, when I came to sell the property, I found that other buyers were not as keen on it as I was and so I had to sell the property at a loss.

Step seven – Rent and sell

Your agent will have identified tenants for you and if all goes to plan, your tenants will be paying you rent that will meet the mortgage payments. You may find that you will have to meet the first one or two mortgage payments yourself until the tenants are in place, and so you should build this potential cost into your budget.

It is now important that you value the property on a regular basis. The intention is to sell the property once it has realized a real gain equal that which is less than you annual capital gains allowance, as noted above. Once it has, sell it! Remember this is a business and you must not fall in love with the property. To avoid tax liabilities you should turn around the properties regularly. If your IFA will not help you with the workings and arrangements with regard to capital gains tax then get another one that will. You don't want an adviser who only sells you things, you want one that will advise and this means on any financial matter.

Step eight – Use multiple properties

If you are going to be involved with property purchase it is a very sensible idea to spread the risk involved in your purchases. I, therefore, believe that, "all things being equal" it is better to own two properties for £50,000 each than one for £100,000. Holding two properties will give you more flexibility as well as reducing the potential risk of the venture.

You should aim to build up a string of properties which you can sell and rotate on an ongoing basis. By doing this you will keep your cash flow moving, which will help to reduce the general risk of property purchase.

Using OPM to accelerate your plan is dangerous but can be very rewarding when it works. If you spend time on it, then it can produce financial independence within three to five years, but this will take some serious work and commitment on your part. It is not something to enter into and 'tinker' with. It needs total dedication to get right, as well as a steady nerve!

I am a firm believer that everyone should have some property within their capital portfolio, but only as an accelerating asset. I do not think it should be held for the sake of it. If you want to hold property for the long term I recommend that you use one of the many property funds offered by the investment houses. These will give you professional management at a fraction of the cost of owning your own property, as well as giving you more liquidity and flexibility.

Chapter 13   Destroying the Debt

Debt can be one of the greatest barriers to financial Independence. I have found that debt can be both a benefit and a curse depending on your own personal circumstances, the way in which you have built debt and how you are using it. Debt in itself is not a bad thing if it is used correctly, for the right reasons at the right times. The problems stem from using it incorrectly, for the wrong reasons and in the wrong way.

Having said that, there are two broad differences between good debt and bad, understanding the difference will give you an idea of how you stand. The purpose of this chapter is to enable you to establish if you have debt problems, and to show you a tried and tested system to get you out of debt. Of course the real trick, once you have got out of debt, is staying out of debt!

Good Debt

It can be considered that no debt is good. If you owe money and are paying out interest to a third party then how can it be good? The point here is that debt can be good if it aids your plan to Financial Independence. If your debt will actively improve your financial plan and build Financial Independence quicker than without it, then it can be a good thing. That is provided that it is done in the right way at the right time.

Generally speaking there are 5 types of debt or circumstances when debt can be considered good. They are as follows:

1. Tax Deduction

2. Rate vs Return

3. Low Rate

4. Gearing

5. Property Purchase

Tax Deduction

This is probably the best form of debt, a debt that is a tax right-off. In the chapter entitled More Saving I discussed the idea of using a business to reduce your tax liability. In this I showed how a loan, used for business purposes is tax deductible and thus reduces your tax liability which means that, in effect, the taxman is paying the interest for you. I recommend that all clients retain any debt that is tax deductible rather than clear the debt. You may be in circumstances where you have sufficient funds to clear the debt, but if it is tax deductible, then you will be better off keeping the cash and investing it rather than clearing the debt, as to do so will simply increase your tax liability.

Rate vs Return

This is a simple concept and it is surprising how often this situation happens in the business world. Put simply, debt is good if the interest rate that you are paying to the lender is lower than the rate of return that you can get on your investments.

For example in August 1999 it was possible to borrow at a rate of 8.9% APR. This meant that on a loan of £10,000 you would pay interest over one year of £563.42. If you had invested this money in shares in Lloyds TSB shares on August 23rd you would have purchased each share for £8.44 each, selling them two days later you would have obtained £9.03

per share, the gain being 7%. This would have produced a gross profit of £700, less the interest of £563.42, giving a net profit of £136.58 in two days! This means that you would have covered your interest for a year and made additional income of £136.58.

A word of warning, borrowing to invest is a high-risk activity but for some people it can be a great way to accelerate a financial plan. I look at this in more detail in the chapter on Investing.

Low Rate

Competition in business is fierce and nowhere more so than in the financing business. Most banks and lending institutions have separate lending arms, which arrange financing for shops and other retail outlets. The name of the game here is volume. Once they have a customer 'on the books' they can then cross sell and start to make money. The problem is, getting the customer on board and to do this they have to enter into arrangements with shops and retail outlets to offer their finance facilities. They will offer the retailer a commission for selling the finance, but the greatest volumes of business are through the national chain retailers and to attract these retailers better packages must be offered. It is for this reason that you see many shops offering 'interest free credit'. Unfortunately, there is a difference between genuine interest free and cross-subsidized interest free credit. Cross-subsidized interest free credit occurs where a price for a product is artificially increased to pay for the cost of the finance. This means that the interest rate is built into the cost of the goods and you, in effect end up paying the interest indirectly. This activity has been outlawed, but still goes on in some retailers and you should watch for it.

Genuine interest free credit, is, however, a good form of debt. A fine example occurred in 1997, when Vauxhall motors offered their 50/50 deal. With this deal you paid a 50% deposit on the car and then had twelve months interest free before you had to pay the remaining balance on the car. If you had purchased a car for say £14,000 you would pay £7000 immediately and £7000 in one years time. At that time the typical interest that you would have received from a bank or building society was 6.25%, this means that you would have made £455 in the course of a year for the privilege of having the debt.

Gearing

Gearing is covered in detail in the chapter on Accelerating Your Plan and so I will not go into too much detail now.

Gearing is the process of accelerating return by using other people's money, an example would be when you buy a house using a mortgage. You may buy a house for £100,000 and pay a deposit of £10,000 leaving a mortgage of £90,000. If you sold the house a year later for £105,000 your gain would be £5,000, or 5% of the initial price of the house. But the real gain is actually 50%, as you have made £5000 on your investment of £10,000, in effect you have 'geared' the investment to a higher return. Any loan that you take out for this purpose, providing that it is done properly is 'good debt'.

Property Purchases

Unless you have inherited a great deal of money or have been very fortunate in business, it is unlikely that you will have sufficient money to purchase your own home outright. Like millions of other people you will need to borrow money to purchase a home if you have decided to own a home rather than renting.

There are, of course both advantages and disadvantage to owning your own home, I believe that it is important to buy your own home. Firstly, because it gives you a greater sense of security when you own a property (that is provided that you are covered by the relevant insurances), and secondly because ultimately you will own the home without a mortgage and so will require less capital to become Financially Independent.

I therefore recommend to all clients that when the time is right they purchase their own home which will involve borrowing on a mortgage which is 'good debt' provided that:

- You borrow less than you can comfortably afford to repay.

- Your repayments, if increased to an interest rate of 12%, would still be affordable.

- You protect your payments with sufficient permanent health insurance, life cover and critical illness insurance. I do not recommend the use of accident and sickness insurance, as this is over priced and is not as effective as permanent health insurance. I also do not usually recommend redundancy insurance and this is for two reasons. Firstly, it is extremely expensive, and often has a great deal of 'small print' which can affect the payout of a policy.

Disadvantages of Good Debt

There is a psychological downside even to good debt, even if the interest on a debt is tax deductible, it is still a debt and it can affect your belief system and, in effect, work against you. For this reason it is important to decide early on, if you are happy to have debt or not. Some people feel better without debt regardless of which type they have, others, on the other hand, are not affected psychologically by debt at all. You must decide which type you are and use this to for the foundation of your decisions regarding debt.

Bad Debt

So what is bad debt? At the risk of saying the obvious, anything that is not good debt!

In particular bad debt usually comes from people overspending and living beyond their means. Prior to becoming an IFA, I was Manager of an American bank which lent money to people in the UK. Our job was to persuade people to borrow our money, often at extremely high rates of interest. I am still amazed, when I think back, at the amount and purposes for which people would borrow money. We would have people borrow for Christmas, holidays, birthdays or just shopping and many other short-term reasons!

I am not saying that you should not borrow, although, once you have built your Capital Account you should not need to borrow from anyone else but yourself again, but I am saying that you should be very careful what you borrow money for.

I recommend that you only borrow money if it is for one of the reasons noted earlier or for extremely large capital purchases, for example a car. Unless you have built your Capital Account it is unlikely that you will have sufficient money to spend on a £10,000 car, and so you will have to borrow. But if you are going to borrow think how much it will really cost you. Let me give you an example

How much does that car really cost?

I had a client who liked cars, I mean he really liked cars! He was one of those people who had to change his car every two to three years, each time he changed, he bought another brand new car and part exchanged his existing car, taking the remainder on finance. Because of this he always had to make a car finance payment, in his case about £700 per month and yet he was only saving £200 per month, because that was all he could 'afford'. So how much was this costing him? Well it is obvious that it was costing him £700 per month, but think for a moment. If he decided to stick with one of the cars he bought he would then have £700 per month to save or invest. If invested in a simple tracking unit trust this figure would have built over say 20 years to just under £1 million! This means that his car had cost him a little over £970,000. Now that's an expensive car!

Of course, we must live in the real world and we must understand that we will have the need to make significant purchases and will need to borrow, but provided we are sensible, and borrow at realistic interest rate (anything under 10% APR is probably acceptable), over short time periods, then we will not get into trouble.

Unfortunately, this is not the case for many people, they get into financial difficulties, by over borrowing. They run-up credit card bills and other small retail debts and find it very hard to get out of the habit of borrowing. Once they have to make large loan repayments it becomes increasingly hard to stop the bus and get off!

If you are one of these people, then you must change things now. You will not become even moderately wealthy, let alone seriously wealthy, unless you control and ultimately rid yourself of this debt.

How to rid yourself of debt

There are three ways to rid yourself of debt:

1. Consolidation

2. Arrangement

3. Bankruptcy

Consolidation

Consolidation means getting all your debts under one roof. It means taking a larger loan to clear all your smaller loans. This can work if done correctly but I strongly recommend that you seek the advice of your IFA before doing so.

The first thing to consider is the rate that you will arrange the consolidation loan at, and then secondly, the term of the loan.

If you need to take a consolidation loan then you are probably going to borrow a substantial sum. It is important that you borrow sufficient money to clear ALL the outstanding debts and roll them into one single payment. In my experience, it does not work if you do not consolidate all the debts, you must clear them all and start afresh. Because you will be borrowing a significant sum you should be able to obtain a better rate of interest than with many smaller debts. This is an area where your IFA will help and he will be able to tell you the lowest cost lender for the amount that you want to borrow and will provide details of that lender. If the IFA cannot do this for you then you should consider changing your IFA as this is a vital part of Financial Planning, and a good adviser will have this information easily to hand.

The term that you select must be a term that will enable you to clear the debts in reasonable time, but will still allow you to save a portion of your income. You see, it is no good saying to yourself, "I will clear all my debts then I'll save", because in practice this does not work. What will happen is that some other form of expenditure will crop up and you will not have any funds to pay for it and so you will borrow again. This is why you must still save at the same time as repaying the debt. Therefore choose a sensible term, even if it is a little longer than you wanted, so that can leave some disposable income to save.

Arrangement

An arrangement, is an agreement with your creditors to repay the amount owed over a longer period, perhaps with a reduction or suspension of the interest payments.

This is one of the oldest ways to clear debt, but is still one of the most effective. It is recommended by both Licensed Debt Councilors and the Citizens Advice Bureau. If used correctly you can use it to avoid legal action and bankruptcy. That is not to say that it is easy, it is very simple, but it will take some effort on your part to get it to work correctly. An arrangement with creditors is simply a promise to pay the creditors based upon the proportion of debt that you have, the largest getting the largest payment, the smallest debt the smallest payment.

To make an arrangement complete the following:

1. Complete a full and accurate income and expenditure list. This must include all your regular payments together with your irregular expenses such as clothing etc. The list must not, however, include your debtors/creditors. This income should also include a savings figure and as with consolidation, you must start saving and if you do not start saving now, then you will not break the habit of borrowing. At the bottom of the list, deduct from the income the expenses to give you a disposable income.

2. Draw up a list of all your creditors detailing exactly how much you owe each of them and be sure to include details such as addresses and account numbers. Total up the debts and the divide each debt by the total of the debts and multiply by 100. This will give the proportion of each debt and list this alongside the debts, together with the amount that this represents based upon your disposable income.

For example:

Any Town Bank	£5000	50%	£100
Credit card	£2500	25%	£50
Car Loan	£2000	20%	£40
Shop account	£500	5%	£10
Total	**£10,000**	**100%**	**£200**

3. Write to each of the creditors explaining your situation and including both of these two schedules and offer to make regular payments to them, dictated by these calculations.

You will find that 99% of all creditors will accept this arrangement, and in addition you will find that 80% of them will also agree to reduce or stop charging interest while you make the payments. This is because this arrangement is very similar to those that would be made by a County Court, but without the time and expense that Court action would involve. In the event of a creditor failing to accept this arrangement I suggest that you refer to the local Citizens Advice Bureau who will than take the matter up on your behalf.

That this system works only if you keep to it. You will, over a course of a few months, find that you are receiving no more threatening telephone calls or reminder letters, and so sleeping better at night, and you will begin to build a Capital Account.

Bankruptcy

This is the last and most extreme way to rid yourself of debt. It involves drawing a line under your finances and starting again. You can only file for bankruptcy, once someone has taken you to court, and if you, and your creditors circumstances will be best served by taking this action.

You do not need a solicitor or lawyer to file for bankruptcy, but I do recommend that you use an Insolvency Practitioner, or a Licensed Debt Councillor. Their fees will be added to the debt, and will be taken as a priority. However, a word of warning, this is a last resort, and you should only go down this route if you have tried firstly consolidation and secondly an arrangement.

Summary

It is vital that you rid yourself of debt as quickly as you can but this must not be at the cost of saving. You must ensure that you save whatever your circumstances but it does not matter how much you save, although more would be better than less, but you must save. Even if you have large debts and have made an arrangement with you creditors, you must still build into your budget sufficient funds to save towards building your Capital Account. Remember that your capital account will be your emergency fund, it will be the fund from which you will borrow should the need arise Unless you begin to build your capital account you will never break the cycle of borrowing.

Chapter 14   Summary

If you have read this book in order, you will now be ready to put your plan into operation.

By completing the exercises in "the WHY" you will have built the belief system that you will require to become seriously wealthy, even on your salary. However, you will need to top this up on occasions to develop the belief system fully.

By completing the exercises "the HOW" you will now know what constitutes being really wealthy, in particular what constitutes Financial Independence. You will also know the constituent parts that build towards Financial Independence and the factors involved in developing your financial plan through savings, investments and debt control.

Now comes the important part: TAKING ACTION.

When all is said and done, it all comes down to one thing, 'taking action'. You can read as much as you like, believe what you like, but unless you actually take some action nothing will happen. I believe that if you have built the correct belief structure, then this in itself will ensure that you actually take action. Someone who has the right belief system will be the type of person that takes the correct action. This is why it is so important to build the right beliefs.

You must consider what action you have taken. If you have not completed the exercises or read this book in the correct order, then what do you intend to do now?

If you have not taken the suggested advice so far then start right now. Set aside some time to do the work that is required. It is so very easy to become wealthy and then Financially Independent, it just takes some effort, and this is the real reason why people do not achieve their goals.

With the aid of this book you can set your goals, you can quantify them precisely, and set out the time line that you want to work within. I believe that the average person can achieve Financial Independence within 20 years, if they can accept a little risk on their investments. It will take perhaps 15 years if you are prepared to sacrifice a little, 10 years if you are fortunate with some of your investments. Most people in the UK never become financially secure, let alone Independent. In fact most people in the UK are one pay-cheque away from financial ruin. Is this how you want to be? Do you want to rely on the state for support in the future? Do you want to be at someone else's beck and call? Or do you want to be master of your own destiny?

Imagine what it would be like to be Financially Independent. You can do whatever it is that you want to do. You can spend your time however you want to spend it. You can help whoever you want to help. Just imagine the good causes you could support, both with your time and money. But you can only do this if you are financially secure first, and it's so easy to get that way, all it takes is a little time and effort.

So why not decide.

- Decide now that you are going to be Financial Independent. Decide that you will do whatever it takes to be independent of other people.

- Decide to set aside the time to draft up your plan, and commit to save and invest to protect yourself and your family.

- Decide for yourself what protection products you must put in place, to ensure that you will survive financially no matter what happens.

- Decide what you need to keep in your Capital Account to protect yourself from financial emergencies and debt.

- Calculate what you need to keep in your Income Account to ensure that, come what may you will be able to survive financially for a minimum of one year.

- Understand that the money that you hold in your Income Account must be used to work for you. If invested well it will start earning for you, and then it will earn even more again.

- Decide how much you will save regularly, and that you will never reduce that amount.

- Agree with yourself that you will review the amount that you save, and will increase that amount every 90 days, no matter how small.

- Commit to save half, and spend half of all additional income that you receive to ensure that you will enjoy the benefits of your income, both now and in the future.

- Agree with yourself, what you need to be Financially Independent, and decide to achieve it.

- If you take these actions, and consistently work to achieve your goals, you will become Financially Independent, and SERIOUSLY RICH ON MY INCOME